FAMOUS
AMERICAN HORSES

BOOKS BY FREDERICK L. DEVEREUX, JR.

FAMOUS AMERICAN HORSES

21 Steeplechasers, Trotters, Cowponies, Hunters,
Flat Racers, Show Horses and Battle Mounts
That Have Made History

by
FREDERICK L. DEVEREUX, JR.

With drawings by
TRAN MAWICKE

THE DEVIN-ADAIR COMPANY • OLD GREENWICH, CONNECTICUT

ISBN No. 0-8159-5512-X
Library of Congress Catalog Card Number: 75-13347

Manufactured in the U.S.A.

Preface

No one book can possibly hope to include all the horses deserving to be called famous. *Famous American Horses* is necessarily a selective work, presenting the accomplishments of a handful of remarkable horses that have contributed to American history—either in sport, war or in the pre-machine age when the horse was the major means of transportation. It has been a difficult task to narrow the field to a workable number of entries, and the reader should understand that the purpose has been to include a wide range of horse activity—outstanding exploits in racing, steeplechasing, horse shows, rodeo, cavalry and Indian campaigns, historical rides and many other interesting, useful purposes to which Americans have put their horses.

Early writers, particularly the poets, glamorize their heroes and exaggerate their feats. Until recently, when much early Americana has been crowded out of the classroom by the necessity of learning to cope with the nuclear age, every schoolboy was familiar with Sheridan's ride and the midnight ride of Paul Revere. Although the familiar legends bear little relation to the actual events, the facts are often more interesting than the legends. Research for this work uncovered many conflicting reports to challenge and many improbable feats to examine. As a horseman, I have used my best judgment to eliminate the improbable and to select the most likely.

The facilities of the Boston and New York Public Libraries, as well as the Norman Williams Public Library of Woodstock, were invaluable sources of information in compiling this book. I am appreciative of the superb illustrations provided by Tran Mawicke, who has painstakingly striven for, and achieved, great accuracy. And, finally, I am most grateful to Mary Fraser, without whose cheerful cooperation *Famous American Horses* would never have seen the light of day.

Frederick L. Devereux, Jr.

Woodstock, Vermont

To the memory of
RANGER
grandson of Man o' War

The best horse I ever rode

Contents

FAMOUS
AMERICAN HORSES

I
Paul Revere's Narragansett Pacer

At the time of the American Revolution, the Narragansett Pacer was unquestionably the most popular saddle horse in America and the West Indies. One in particular was destined to be immortalized in Henry Wadsworth Longfellow's poem, *Paul Revere's Ride*. Stanzas of "the midnight ride," committed to memory by generations of school children, depict a wild gallop from Boston to Concord "through every Middlesex village and farm" to warn that "the British are coming!"

Unfortunately, history has omitted to record the name of Paul's mount, but we do know that it was a chestnut mare of small size but good quality lent to him by Deacon Larkin of Charlestown, across the river from Boston. According to Revere's report, Deacon Larkin selected a Narragansett mare for the projected trip.

Not many people today know that little Rhode Island was once the leading state in the breeding of horses, producing more each year than Virginia, Kentucky or Maryland—the three states generally credited with being the major producers of horseflesh in the early days of America's history. The lush countryside and good climate from Point Judith north toward Providence were ideal for raising horses, and the large pastures bounded by the Atlantic Ocean, Narragansett Bay and the rivers and creeks flowing into them, could contain horses with only a minimum of fencing to control movement.

The Rhode Islanders developed a useful breed of light horse, mostly chestnut and somewhat on the small side, whose good disposition, great endurance, good manners and ambling gait made it a pleasant mount to ride. Because of the dominance of Narragansett Bay in the area, these horses came to be known as Narragansett Pacers, although many of them did not develop the pacer's peculiar "side-wheeler" gait whereby both legs on the same side advance at the same time.

In the mid-1770's, before the American Revolution, the Narragansett Pacer was much in demand in the Caribbean area, where the planters valued them as mounts from which to supervise

11

labor in the sugarcane fields. At that time Newport, Rhode Island, was a leading seaport specializing in the importation of rum from the islands of Jamaica, Puerto Rico, and in particular, Barbados; hence it was a natural exchange that kept the ships loaded in both directions—to export horses to the islands and return with rum distilled from sugarcane. As a consequence, the export of Narragansett Pacers became a big business, with many breeding farms raising a thousand or more horses each year for the combined domestic and export markets.

The Narragansett Pacer is today an extinct breed, a victim of the mechanization which allowed conversion of grazing land to other purposes. As Rhode Island grew in population and industry, the horse breeding industry gradually faded out, and by the time of the Civil War had almost vanished.

Before the outbreak of the American Revolution, Paul Revere, a noted Boston silversmith, was an active member of the Committee of Safety, a group of prominent Massachusetts men who were opposed to George III's heavy-handed treatment of the American colonies. By April of 1775, tension between the citizens of Boston and the British force occupying the city was running high and the Committee of Safety was planning to send delegates, including Samuel Adams and John Hancock, to the newly organized Continental Congress at Philadelphia.

Meanwhile an allied group of revolutionaries, the minutemen, were hoarding cannon, powder and other military supplies at Concord in anticipation of armed conflict with the British. By April 18, Dr. John Warren, head of the Committee of Safety, had learned from friendly servants at British headquarters that the British had knowledge of the Concord arms cache and were planning an expedition to seize these stores and at the same time capture and imprison Adams and Hancock, who were staying in nearby Lexington.

It was known that the raiding party would move during the night of the eighteenth—first to Lexington and then to Concord—but the route was not known to Warren. There were two alternate routes, the longer one by land and a shorter one by an amphibious crossing of the Charles River followed by a land march to the two towns. At ten o'clock that night British troops in full marching gear formed on Boston Common, and Dr. Warren knew that he must make haste to alert Adams, Hancock and the minutemen.

Believing that the most probable line of advance would be by the land route, Warren dispatched Samuel Dawes to proceed in that direction to alert the countryside. Dawes' primary mission was to warn Adams and Hancock of their possible capture, with orders then to proceed to Concord to inform the friendly forces there of the British expedition. Paul Revere was selected by Warren to stand by in Charlestown in case the British forces should come that way. His instructions were to cross over to Charlestown, borrow a horse and watch for a signal from the North Church belfry, where the sexton would display one lantern if the British were following Dawes overland, or two if they were crossing the Charles River.

Revere was rowed across the Charles by two friends, and his boat passed under the stern of the British man-of-war *Somerset* without challenge. Gaining the opposite shore, he went to the house of his friend Larkin to borrow a horse for the ride. Later he reported to the Committee of Safety that Deacon Larkin had provided him with a small Narrangansett mare.

Shortly after eleven o'clock, two lights were observed in the church belfry, and Paul Revere took off for Lexington. Contrary to Longfellow's glamorized version, the ride, if it was not a fiasco, was at least a comedy of errors—as we gather from Revere's own account of the incident.

Fortunately, the moon was almost full and rising, providing good visibility. As Revere walked and occasionally trotted his mare toward Medford, he noticed a two-man British outpost blocking the road ahead and turned north to avoid them. Almost at once he was spotted, and the enemy came after him in hot pursuit. At this point Revere put the mare to a gallop for about three hundred yards—apparently the only time that night when he rode at more than a trot. The British pursuit lasted for only a few seconds because the leading rider fell into a pond and his companion stopped to assist him.

Without further incident Paul Revere continued his ride, mostly at a walk to judge by the time of his arrival at Lexington where he met Samuel Dawes, who had left Boston earlier by the longer route. Together they roused Adams and Hancock and loafed in Lexington for about half an hour before starting down the road to Concord. They could hardly have paused for that half-hour to rest their horses, for they averaged less than five miles an hour en route to Lexington—a very slow pace indeed (a horse's normal walk is four miles an hour). More likely they felt little sense of urgency, assuming that the British must be several hours behind them because of the time it would take to move across the Charles in small boats.

Shortly after departing from Lexington, Revere and Dawes fell in with Dr. Samuel Prescott—a fortunate meeting for the revolutionary cause, it shortly developed. Dr. Prescott, an ardent patriot, was on his way home to Concord and welcomed the opportunity to ride in company. He was told of the British raid and asked to help alert householders along the way, which he readily agreed to do.

About two o'clock on the morning of the nineteenth, the three riders were halfway between Lexington and Concord when Dawes pulled up to alert the occupants of a house set well back from the road, while Revere and Prescott rode on for a short distance. Suddenly a four-man British outpost halted the two and forced them into an apple orchard. Prescott watched for an opportunity to break loose and, when his captor relaxed his hold on the bridle, put spurs to his horse, jumped a stone wall and escaped. Revere attempted to take advantage of the confusion by heading for a nearby wood. Instead he ran into six British troopers backstopping the outpost and was captured. Dawes, unobserved by the British, took off at a gallop toward Concord, but fell off his horse near the outpost and was also captured.

Revere and Dawes, the two messengers of freedom who had set out to warn the Concord minutemen of the impending British attack, now found themselves captive, their ride ended in fruitless ignominy. To add further insult, the commander of the British detachment, Major Mitchell of the Fifth Regiment of Grenadiers, commandeered the Narragansett mare for one of his sergeants. The last we know of Deacon Larkin's favorite mount is that she was ridden down the road toward Concord by a British soldier, as Paul Revere and Samuel Dawes were turned loose by their captors and ordered to walk back to Lexington. They returned with their mission to alert the people of Concord unaccomplished.

Fortunately for the revolutionary cause, Doctor Prescott, on the ride purely by accident, galloped cross-country and warned the minutemen of British intentions so that, shortly after sunrise, the British were routed at the North Bridge by the minutemen who "fired the shot heard 'round the world," and started the American Revolution.

II
Nelson

George Washington's Hunter

Contrary to popular belief, and to the way he has been depicted by most painters, George Washington's charger Nelson was not white. Washington rode many horses in battle, whose names are not remembered, but the mount that was to remain with him throughout the war and live to survive him, was his favorite hunter Nelson—a big-boned, light chestnut gelding.

"First in war, first in peace, first in the hearts of his countrymen." What American does not recognize this familiar saying about George Washington, first President of the United States? Other Washington firsts come to the minds of horsemen. He was first to import Spanish and French jackasses and mate them with local mares to produce a strain of large mules for farm work, and he was the first master of foxhounds in Virginia.

A horse that was Washington's pride and joy was called Magnolia, a Thoroughbred stallion that stood at stud in Mount Vernon from 1785 through 1788. It had been Washington's ambition after the Revolution to become the new nation's preeminent breeder and owner of racehorses, but this ambition was never realized. Magnolia is known to have lost a match race at Alexandria, Virginia, to a roan colt owned by Thomas Jefferson. So far as can be determined, this race is the only recorded event in which a racehorse owned by a President of the United States ran against one owned by a future President. Apparently after Magnolia's defeat Washington decided to abandon racing, for the stallion was shortly sold to "Light-Horse Harry" Lee, America's first cavalry commander during the Revolution, and the band of more than a hundred unbroken colts and fillies at Mount Vernon was dispersed. It is interesting to note that in reality Magnolia's sale was more of a trade, with Washington giving Lee the stallion in exchange for five thousand acres of Kentucky land.

George Washington was an avid sportsman, and fox hunting was one of his favorite pursuits. At Mount Vernon he maintained a large pack of imported English foxhounds and a stable of hunters to mount the many visitors who came there for the sport. The rolling country on the banks of the Potomac River offered good galloping ground and an abundance of foxes for the chase. Obstacles were similar to those found today in Virginia—stone walls and post-and-rail fencing. Washington's carefully kept diary reveals that his favorite hunter Nelson was a gift from Governor Thomas Nelson, Jr., of Virginia. Because the gelding was not a Thoroughbred, nothing is known of his breeding, but he must have been a half-bred or better to carry Washington's weight of 200 pounds cross-country at speed for a hard day's hunting. A master of foxhounds must be superbly mounted if he is to give the field a good day's sport, so it may be assumed that Nelson was well muscled, a good mover, an excellent jumper and a horse with both great endurance and a calm disposition. As Washington selected from a large stable, we can further assume that Nelson was a comfortable horse to ride and was well mannered.

Nelson was given to Washington as a three-year-old and was hunted for the next ten years until the outbreak of the American Revolution temporarily suspended such pleasant pastimes as fox hunting. When Washington was commissioned Commander in Chief of the Rebel force, he left Philadelphia—then the capital of the new country—for Boston to lead the troops engaged in fighting the British. Always a man of action, Washington declined to travel by coach and rode Nelson, the horse that was to serve him faithfully throughout the long war—from New England to the Carolinas.

There are so many unfounded legends about Washington that it becomes difficult to distinguish Nelson from his other mounts. No one horse could have carried him daily throughout the war and it is known that several of Washington's mounts died of fatigue. History records, for example, that one horse died under the General at the Battle of Trenton after a long day spent galloping up and down the lines to rally and direct the Continental troops. There must have been many such weary days—too many for any one horse to survive. Nelson, however, was always the Commander's first choice as a mount and the gallant chestnut was the only horse to be with him throughout the long conflict.

With Washington, Nelson endured the miserable winter at Valley Forge, where half-starved men and horses shivered in the cold and scrounged for kernels of corn. A leader of great moral character, Washington declined to take advantage of the comforts his wealth could easily have obtained; rather he insisted that he and Nelson share the troops' discomfort and live no better than they did. When spring finally came, bringing warmer weather and relieving the shortage of food, the old war horse was still carrying Washington throughout the camp on his daily inspections, and cross-country to the outposts.

The Battle of Yorktown in October 1781 ended the Revolution. When Lord Cornwallis, the British commander, surrendered his force, the long hostilities were over and the establishment of a new nation was assured. The redcoats marched out to lay down their arms while, appropriately, their band played "The World Turned Upside Down."

Washington, mounted on Nelson, accepted the surrender. The General and his horse had

come a long way together since the ride from Philadelphia to Boston, and they still had a long way to go. Nelson was often ridden by Washington during his terms as President.

As a footnote to history it is interesting that there is no true likeness of Nelson in any of the artists' creations that have been preserved. The white chargers prancing furiously under Washington's firm hand are all figments of the artists' imagination.

III
Prince Charlie

*Who Saved
Thomas Jefferson
from Capture
by the British*

Captain Jack Jouett, of the Virginia Militia, needed a weight-carrying horse with endurance and the ability to move boldly and surely cross-country. Jouett was commander of a troop of cavalry continuously engaged in skirmishes and rear-guard actions against the British. These were crack British forces under a superb commander, Colonel Banastre Tarleton, and the Americans had to be well-mounted in order to be effective against superior enemy forces and equipment.

Fortunately, Virginia was the breeding center for fine blooded hunters, and Captain Jouett found a large-boned bay at a farm near his father's farm in Louisa County. The bay carried the captain's 220 pounds confidently and smoothly under all kinds of difficult campaign conditions. Jouett's mount, Prince Charlie, was the envy of all other troopers and a source of pride and affection to his owner.

There was a lull in the fighting in the spring of 1781 and many patriots had secured leave to visit home and attend to private affairs. Thomas Jefferson, Governor of Virginia and author of the Declaration of Independence, was at his home—Monticello—near Charlottesville. Captain Jouett, sixty miles away at Louisa Courthouse, had stopped at the Cuckoo Tavern for refreshment before proceeding to his father's nearby farm for a family visit. It was a rainy night in June, and the captain decided to wait out the rain at the bar. He put Prince Charlie in the tavern's stable to be groomed and fed.

Shortly before midnight, Jouett heard horses approaching the tavern in considerable number. Knowing there was no American force in the vicinity, he slipped out a side door and hid in the bushes, keeping the entrance to the tavern in view. Before long, two British cavalrymen appeared, soon followed by a full troop. The men dismounted and, careless of security at that late hour in the rain, took their ease on the tavern porch and in the bar. Jouett was close enough to overhear the officer in charge conferring with his subordinates and, to his consternation, learned that the enemy force's mission was to raid Monticello and other estates near Charlottesville and to surprise and capture Jefferson and several other dignitaries of the Continental Congress.

Jouett had no choice but to remain hidden and quiet until the British force had mounted and moved out down the road to Charlottesville sixty miles away. He knew that they could not hope to reach their destination much before mid-morning. After what seemed an interminable length of time, the last British set of fours in the column departed, and Jouett ran swiftly to the tavern stable where he saddled and bridled Prince Charlie in the dark. The captain followed the British troop down the road at a discreet but alert distance. The rain was in favor for shadowing the enemy; he knew that he must get ahead of them and beat them to Monticello if Jefferson was to be warned in time.

As he trailed along in the dark, Jouett considered the difficulties: there was no hope of passing through the enemy column on the only direct road to Charlottesville, and he would have to go cross-country—over a longer more hazardous route in the rain and dark. But it had to be done. The big question was whether Prince Charlie could handle the unfamiliar course over logs, fences and ditches; through gullies, thickets and scrub trees. A cross-country ride in daylight, picking one's way, can be dangerous at speed, but a night ride across the same country is a far more difficult trip.

Finally Jack Jouett made his decision. The trip must be attempted, and it must be successful if the Revolution was not to be endangered by the capture of Jefferson and the others. He and Prince Charlie must run the danger of a broken leg or neck in the attempt, and they must get through. He would follow the enemy until a favorable trail was reached—one that could be taken cross-country to avoid the British. Meanwhile he would remain behind the enemy column, close enough to keep it under observation, but not so close as to attract attention.

About ten miles down the road, an hour and a half after leaving Cuckoo Tavern, the British commander called a rest halt. By this time the rain had subsided and the moon was beginning to shed some light on the terrain. Jouett was in familiar territory and decided to start his cross-country trip, taking advantage of the better weather conditions and the resting enemy force. Leaving the road, he put Prince Charlie over a low stone wall and galloped behind a row of trees screening him from the British. He trotted up and over a nearby ridge to a stream line in the next valley and followed it until he reached a familiar wagon trail. Once on the rutted trail, he took up a hand gallop and was off on one of the most arduous rides in history.

After a few miles the trail petered out. Jouett and Prince Charlie trotted through brambles, up and down hill, until another path was found. Galloping again, the pair forded streams, jumped fallen trees and continued their urgent mission. By this time Jouett's face was a mass of scratches from barbed bushes and low-hanging branches. He was to carry scars from some of these cuts as long as he lived. But he was a tough, accomplished horseman, superbly mounted for this effort, and both man and horse were making good the reputation they had earned in combat against the British.

Twice Prince Charlie fell in unseen ditches; each time the gallant thoroughbred scrambled out and went on. And so the mad ride continued, on trails where they could be found and cross-country between the trails. Few men could have made such a ride under those conditions and fewer horses could have completed it and survived the effort. None of the modern-day endurance rides, for which man and mount carefully prepare with conditions and routes well known in advance, can begin to compare with Prince Charlie's transport of Jack Jouett on that wild sixty-mile nighttime cross-country ride to Charlottesville. Probably it was the most difficult feat of horsemanship known to history.

Shortly after dawn, and well ahead of the British, Captain Jouett and Prince Charlie arrived at Monticello—bloody, wet and close to exhaustion. Jefferson was roused by Jouett's impatient knocking at the door and listened with skepticism, but very soon a neighbor arrived with confirmation that the British were indeed coming, and Jefferson took his telescope and located the redcoats galloping up the mountain toward Monticello. There was now no doubt that Jouett's incredible ride had been in earnest. Jefferson quickly sent his family off to a neighboring estate, and took to the woods himself, on horseback.

Where Jouett and Prince Charlie went after alerting Mr. Jefferson is not known, but it must have been to a friend's nearby home, where Prince Charlie could be rubbed down and rested. Certainly Captain Jouett needed a good sleep as well as attention to his cuts. Shortly thereafter, the pair were back in active service with the cavalry, where they remained until the conclusion of the war, harassing the enemy in countless engagements.

It is interesting to speculate on the course of American history had Jefferson been captured. Perhaps he might not have become president of the United States. Certainly Virginia would have had to replace him as governor. And the morale of the country would no doubt have suffered if Jouett's ride on Prince Charlie had not thwarted the British raiders and saved Jefferson and the other leaders.

IV
Justin Morgan

*Little Horse
with a
Big Heart*

Vermont's reputation as the most conservative state in the Union is based on a fondness for cherishing and preserving the customs and traditions handed down by earlier generations. One such practice which has endured for more than two centuries—since before the days when Vermont was an independent Republic—is the custom of naming a horse for its first owner, regardless of how many times the animal may have changed hands. One forty-year-old pony, honorably retired to pasture in South Woodstock, was known as Riley by a dozen owners, none of whom had any idea who the original Mr. Riley was or anything else about him other than that he once owned the pony.

Hence, because it happened in Vermont, it is no surprise that the only horse breed to be named after a man is the Morgan; the remarkable stallion that was the foundation sire of the breed and first owned by schoolteacher Justin Morgan of Randolph, Vermont. Because a good Vermonter has a well-developed sense of dignity, he would consider it immodest to name a horse for himself, and it is only after the horse is sold that it is apt to be called by the first owner's name.

Thus schoolteacher Justin Morgan called his colt Figure, and he was only renamed Justin Morgan when Sheriff Rice of Woodstock obtained him in payment of a debt. Thereafter, although he served many masters, he was always known as Justin Morgan.

Justin Morgan (the man) was originally a farmer near Springfield, Massachusetts, and owned a common mare which he bred to a horse named True Briton, a Thoroughbred once owned by General Oliver DeLancey of the British Army, who rode him during the battle of Long Island. While the general was quenching his thirst in a tavern, True Briton was stolen from him by a man named Smith, who took the bay stallion to the American Army at White Plains and sold him to an officer from Hartford. After the war True Briton was leased to a breeder near Springfield, to whom Mr. Morgan sent his mare in 1788. A few months later Morgan moved to Randolph, where he had promise of a less laborious life. His mare was heavy with an unborn foal and, feeling that she

23

should not make the long hard trip north to Randolph, he sold her to a neighbor in Springfield.

Two years later Morgan returned to Springfield in an attempt to collect some money owed him. One of the debtors was his neighbor, who was short of funds and offered True Briton's colt out of the old mare, plus another young horse, in payment of the debt. Morgan accepted the bargain and returned to Randolph, driving a buggy with the yearling colt, Figure, trailing behind.

When Figure was a two-year-old—a very tender age to work an immature horse—Morgan broke him to drive and to ride and also, because of his magnificent conformation, put him at stud. This, too, was most unusual, for stallions are seldom asked to mate with mares until they are fully grown and have proved themselves as outstanding performers; brood-mare owners prefer a stallion of known ability to a green, untried youngster, since the stallion is expected to transmit his proven qualities to the foal.

Even as a two-year-old, with his baby (or "milk") teeth still in his mouth, Figure showed promise of excellence; he was a good looking dark bay with black legs, mane and tail and no white hair; he had wide-set prominent eyes—a sign of intelligence; his coat was fine and glossy; his large sensitive nostrils gave him a spirited expression. His body was exceptionally well put together and heavily muscled; he stood squarely on short legs and moved stylishly at walk, trot and canter. In short, he had power, substance and endurance which, combined with his intelligence, alertness and quiet disposition, made for an exceptionally superior all-purpose horse. At first his small size—he stood just slightly over fourteen hands and weighed 950 pounds—was a mark against him, but he soon proved his worth in competition with much larger horses, and the jibes of "pony horse" soon give way to widespread admiration for the "big little horse," and the "little horse with the big heart."

During his four-year-old year, Morgan leased Figure—still a growing colt—to Robert Evans for $15 to clear fifteen acres of woodland. Evans worked the little stallion long hours at pulling the heavy felled logs and gave him little shelter and poor food. After a long day's work in the woods, Evans was accustomed to taking his ease in the Randolph tavern while tired hungry Figure waited patiently outside in the dark for his master to finish his carousing and take him home.

One winter night Evans overheard another logger telling of the inability of his horse to move a big log from a nearby clearing. Evans bet a gallon of rum that Figure could move the log a distance of fifty-five yards (or ten rods, as distances were measured in those days) with three pulls. The bet was promptly accepted and Figure went to work, digging in his toes and throwing his weight into his collar. He slowly got the log moving and pulled it more than halfway before resting. At this point Evans invited three of the bettors to ride the log the rest of the way and, after a few moments rest, Figure took up the added strain and pulled log and passengers to the agreed-upon mark. From that moment, Figure's fame began to spread, and he became much in demand as a sire who would produce strong, well-muscled horses.

Mr. Morgan died when Figure was a five-year-old and Sheriff William Rice brought him to Woodstock; from that time forward Figure has been known by the name of his original Vermont

master, Justin Morgan, and it is under this second name that his many accomplishments are listed. He was to have ten more owners, almost all of whom worked him very hard. Apparently his owners thought that he was an iron horse—a machine that could never break down, rather than flesh and blood. They all wanted the stud fees that the popular little stallion could command; therefore they entered him in weight-pulling contests, which he invariably won against larger horses, increasing his value as a sire of workhorses. He was entered in trotting races against some of the best competition in the country—not only local New England trotters, but imports from New York and other areas; he won almost all of his important match races against the best trotters of the era, as well as innumerable brushes with local rivals on an impromptu basis.

As a trotter Justin Morgan became one of the leading racers of his day and a much-sought-after sire to improve the breed. His versatility was further demonstrated in flat racing, usually at a quarter of a mile, where he won more than his share of purses at the galloping sport. And finally, Justin Morgan was much in demand as a parade horse, because of his flashy action and spirited demeanor. So great was his fame that President Monroe asked to ride him at the head of a parade in Burlington.

In today's age of specialization, any one of Justin Morgan's five occupations—stallion service, weight-pulling, trotting, flat racing and parading—would be considered a full-time pursuit if excellence was desired. It is remarkable that he could be so versatile and excel at all of them, particularly when he was engaged in farm work—plowing fields and pulling wagons—whenever his owner had no contest, exhibition or visiting mare to attend to.

By the time he was a twenty-year-old, Justin Morgan began to show the strain of two decades of overwork and indifferent care. Instead of being put out to pasture, or given only light work in his declining years as a reward for faithful service, he was sold for a pittance to work in a six-horse team pulling freight up the steep Green Mountain slopes and galloping frantically down the other side of the mountain to avoid being run down by the heavily-loaded wagon.

Finally, when he was in his thirtieth year (the equivalent of a ninety-year-old man) he was so old and thin that he could no longer pull his weight on the freight run and was sent to the farm of Clifford Bean at Chelsea, Vermont, where he was turned out and left to fend for himself, digging for grass through the winter snows, with no shelter from the cold wind. He survived for two more years until, in the bitter winter of 1821, he was kicked by another horse. Bean declined to treat the wound, which became infected, and noble Justin Morgan died of neglect in an icy snowfield. If he had been given proper care in his last ten years, there is no telling how long he might have lived—perhaps even long enough to establish yet another record, this time for longevity among horses. For Justin Morgan's stout heart never faltered despite a lifetime of overwork, underfeeding and general neglect. The wonder is that his disposition did not sour under this treatment. He continued to give his very best, without having to be urged, to all of his many masters throughout his long life. Justin Morgan would be remembered today as a great horse purely on the basis of his spectacular record of meeting the leading horses of his time and outpulling, outwalking, outtrotting and outrunning them. But his greatest claim to enduring fame was as the foundation sire of a new breed of horse, the Morgan; for Justin Morgan had the unique quality of prepotency, the ability to transmit his conformation, strength, endurance, disposition and intelligence to his offspring, regardless of the mare's quality or lack of quality. His sons and daughters were remarkably like their sire in all these respects, and they passed their virtues in turn to their descendants.

Thus a breed of small but hardy utility horse—adaptable both to riding and driving—was developed in the descendants of this one outstanding sire. The present-day Morgan, although somewhat bigger than his remote ancestor, shows the same close-coupled, short-legged, muscular development; is noted for alertness combined with docility and is equally suitable as a family riding or driving general-purpose horse. He is a worthy descendant of the gallant little stallion who carved a niche in the history of Vermont at the turn of the nineteenth century, when horses were thought of primarily as the principal means of transportation and sport.

V
Jeb Stuart's Horses
Civil War Stalwarts

Perhaps the greatest cavalry leader of all time, certainly the "last of the cavaliers," was James Ewell Brown Stuart of the Confederate Army of Northern Virginia. A major general in his early twenties, he caused panic in Washington whenever a rumor reached the War Department that he might be off again on one of his numerous raids behind Union lines. Known as "Beauty" to his West Point classmates (because his face was somewhat less than handsome), Stuart grew a tremendous black beard and became popularly known by the acronym of his initials, "Jeb." Behind the beard lurked a knowing eye for a good horse or a pretty girl.

Jeb Stuart realized almost from the beginning that the Southern cause was lost, and he wrote to his mother that he sought to infuse in his men "the spirit of the chase" as a means of maintaining morale in the face of ultimate defeat. Consequently, his headquarters was a merry one; his orderly, Sweeney, a famous minstrel banjo player, was always on tap for music. Stuart's daringly led expeditions against the plodding Union forces attracted the flower of young Southern manhood—the fox-hunting gentry who viewed mounted combat as a test of courage and horsemanship.

Jeb Stuart was a junior officer in the First U. S. Cavalry Regiment, stationed at Fort Riley in what is now Kansas, when the war clouds broke. A promising career lay ahead of him. He had distinguished himself in combat against the Indians, had married the daughter of his commanding officer and had been recommended for promotion to become the youngest captain in the army. But when Virginia seceded from the Union, he immediately resigned his commission and took up his sword to serve his state.

Stuart's first assignment as a major in the new grey uniform was to report to General Joseph E. Johnson (a ranking officer in the Union army who resigned to assist the Southern cause) at Harper's Ferry in what is now West Virginia. Peppery old Joe was in need of an aggressive horse soldier to break in recruits, and Stuart obliged him by giving them daily contact with the enemy.

Stuart's recruits hit and ran until they became highly proficient in cavalry tactics. Stuart, superbly mounted and the finest horseman in a select group priding itself on horsemanship, was always out in front of his troops—a custom he maintained throughout his career, even when he was a corps commander with seven divisions under his command.

Stuart's first test of leadership was soon to come. The first big battle of the war, Bull Run (or Manassas), was shaping up, and Joe Johnson was ordered to perform a seemingly impossible maneuver—to bring his forces to Manassas and at the same time prevent the larger Union force under General Robert Patterson from going there. He solved this dilemma by ordering Stuart to hold Patterson while he himself disengaged the main body. Stuart (by then a regimental commander) accomplished this by attacking with small forces at a number of points simultaneously— parrying, thrusting, withdrawing and hitting again at another target of opportunity. A confused Patterson, convinced that Johnson was attacking him in force, telegraphed the War Department that he was under attack by superior forces (actually he outnumbered Stuart ten to one) and could not move to reinforce the troops approaching Manassas. When Johnson arrived at Manassas and Stuart knew that Patterson's foot troops, even if unopposed, could not arrive there in time to influence the battle, Stuart made a forced march of twenty-four hours and arrived in time to take a crucial part in turning the Union flank and pursuing the fleeing Northern army. This action brought Stuart to the attention of the high command, and he was promoted to brigadier general and shortly became the eyes, ears and advance striking force of Robert E. Lee's Army of Northern Virginia.

It was important for Stuart to be well mounted and he did not lack quality horseflesh. Of the many fine Thoroughbred hunters that carried him through countless battles, skirmishes and raids, his undoubted favorite was Maryland, a big bay gelding given to him by a female admirer whose name unfortunately is not known. It was Maryland who carried him on the famous ride around General George McClellan, the exploit which so panicked the Union commander that he abandoned his siege of Richmond, the Confederate capital.

General Lee, defending Richmond against McClellan's superior forces, was in the dark concerning the Union's dispositions and strength. He called in Stuart and gave him the rather indefinite mission of probing the right flank of the enemy army. The purpose was to capture prisoners and gather information by observation and raiding—orders which delight a cavalryman's heart, especially when he is given great latitude in their execution. Stuart assembled the crack units of his two regiments and trotted out of Richmond, with Sweeney strumming his favorite campaign tune on the banjo, "If you want to have fun, jine the Cavalry."

After bivouacking undiscovered, Stuart roused his troops before dawn and took off via back country roads, leading the long column of fours toward a supply depot deep in Union territory. Although he captured or overran several small outposts, it was not long before the Union command was alerted that a raiding party was operating at their rear, and a strong cavalry task force under the command of Stuart's father-in-law was sent in pursuit. Stuart had the advantage of knowing the country intimately and the prerogative of choosing the direction of his raid, whereas his father-in-law had to guess at Jeb's intentions and where he might strike next; thus Stuart found himself penetrating ever deeper into the Federal rear to avoid his pursuer.

About noontime he realized that he was halfway around McClellan's army, with the pursuers still following him. He could not retrace his steps and the obvious escape route was to continue on around the enemy, taking more prisoners, burning more supply dumps and causing all the disruption to communications that his troopers could accomplish. And so they continued until the early hours of the next morning, fighting a delaying action to their rear and overrunning the forces blocking their forward progress. Stuart, on Maryland, seemed to be everywhere at once, directing the rear-guard action, leading charges against Federal outposts, encouraging his tired troopers and maneuvering to escape back to the Confederate lines. After a hair-raising fight at a ford in the river separating the two armies, Stuart crossed his troops just in time to avoid capture; he left a wide swath of wrecked wagon trains, burned bridges and useless supply dumps behind him. His troopers were exhausted by the ordeal and Stuart allowed them to rest and recuperate while he rode his tireless horse, Maryland, back to Richmond to report the results of the expedition to General Lee. Meanwhile McClellan concluded that his position was entirely too vulnerable and called off the campaign to seize Richmond—all as a result of Stuart's daring ride.

Stuart's ride gave Confederate morale a great lift, much as Jimmy Doolittle's raid on Tokyo raised American spirits during the dark, early days of World War II. Stuart and Maryland became household words throughout the South. The capture of Richmond, which most military experts agree could have been accomplished by a less excitable general than McClellan, would have been a serious if not fatal blow to the Confederacy.

Although Maryland was Stuart's favorite mount, his cavalry was so continuously active that no one horse could stand the pace, and he had to call on several other superb chargers to carry him from time to time. Two of this string, Lady Margrave, a tall, long-striding chestnut mare, and Skylark (also a gift from a female admirer) were used for the raid on Chambersburg, Pennsylvania. Lee ordered Stuart to undertake this raid for the purpose of capturing Union food and supplies for the underfed and ill-equipped Confederate forces. Lady Margrave and Skylark were ridden on alternate days in this deep probe into enemy territory. Stuart, as was his invariable custom, ranged far and wide up and down his columns, encouraging his troops, supervising the capture of Federal horses and supplies and the destruction of what could not be carried away. All this, of course, was done between intervals of leading charges to disperse and rout the Federal forces converging on the rebel raiders from every direction as the frightened mayors of the besieged towns frantically wired Washington for help. Stuart returned from the Chambersburg raid with hundreds of fat horses and several wagon trains of supplies—clothing, food and money badly needed by the impoverished South. Although the mission was highly successful and added further luster to his distinguished reputation, he was personally despondent. His orderly, "Mulatto Bob," had managed to find a few too many bottles of Pennsylvania rye whiskey and had gone to sleep by the side of the road while tending the two horses. Bob was rudely awakened from his stupor by a

VI
Traveller

*Robert E. Lee's
Favorite Mount,
and "Miss Lucy,"
the General's Mare*

At the time his native state of Virginia seceded from the Union, Robert E. Lee, then a lieutenant colonel, was stationed in Texas. He commanded the First Dragoons, later redesignated the Second U.S. Cavalry regiment. Although offered an important promotion as well as command of the Union forces as replacement for the aging General Winfield Scott, Lee chose to offer his sword to the Southern cause and resigned his commission. In so doing, he became the highest ranking mounted service officer to join the Confederacy.

As commander of the Army of Northern Virginia, Lee's horse-soldiering experience was revealed in a number of ways. His outnumbered cavalry under Jeb Stuart and Wade Hampton consistently outrode and outfought the Federal troopers, and Lee's personal selection of mounts demonstrated his excellent judgment of horseflesh.

To find suitable horses to carry Lee with dependability was not an easy task. He needed an iron horse, one that would not be tiring to ride and one with excellent manners. Furthermore, a general's mount had to be recognized easily by aides and messengers, so distinctive markings were of some importance. But the prime requisites were soundness and good disposition—a mount that could keep going day after arduous day in the field with a minimum of care.

Lee's first horse during the Civil War was a totally unsuitable bay stallion named Richmond, in honor of the citizens of that city, who had presented him with the horse. Although of excellent conformation and breeding, Richmond would not travel quietly in company. He bit and kicked Lee's staff officers' horses and was such a bad actor that Lee quietly rid himself of Richmond as soon as he felt he could do so without offending the well-intentioned donors. His second horse, a roan gelding, was well mannered but did not have the endurance to stand up to the strain of long marches.

At last Lee's cavalry commander, Jeb Stuart, found him a gentle chestnut mare named Lucy Long, to whom the general became quite attached, calling her "Miss Lucy." She stood slightly over fifteen hands, was well built with excellent legs—a "good mover"—and had a very fast walk and an easy canter. With her full mane and tail and thoroughbred-type conformation, she came close to being a model officer's mount. However, Miss Lucy did not have the stamina for extended mounted service. She was more of a pleasure horse than a campaigner, and she had to be used sparingly as an extra, or second, mount.

In 1864, after two years of service, "Miss Lucy" broke down and was sent to a farm in the country where she was captured by a raiding Union cavalry task force. After the war, a friend of General Lee's recognized her in a public riding academy where she was being hired out by the hour; he bought her on the spot and shipped her to Lee's home at Lexington, Virginia, where Mrs. Lee used her as a riding and driving mare. Miss Lucy lived to the ripe old age of thirty-nine when, after having lost all her teeth and being unable to eat, one of the General's sons mercifully chloroformed her.

The one horse to fill the bill in all respects as the commander's first-string mount was an iron-grey gelding of uncertain ancestry. The horse had been named Jeff Davis by his first owner in tribute to the then Secretary of War in the Buchanan cabinet (Davis was later to resign his post with the Federal government and become president of the Confederacy). The grey's second owner had renamed him Greenbrier for the county in what is now West Virginia where he had won several ribbons at the Greenbrier Fair. Lee first saw and admired the grey gelding during a campaign in 1861 in West Virginia; he offered to buy him, but the owner had promised to sell Greenbrier to a Captain Broun and regretfully informed the general that the horse was spoken for. Some months later, while Lee was serving in South Carolina, Captain Broun's outfit arrived there and Lee's interest was again expressed. Broun offered to present the horse to the General, but Lee declined his offer, saying that he would be glad to pay whatever price Captain Broun desired. Broun responded by quoting $175—the price he had paid for the grey, and Lee then insisted on paying $200 to compensate for the war-induced inflation which had lessened the value of the currency.

General Lee soon found that Traveller, as he had renamed his purchase, was exactly what he had been looking for in a top mount. A very strong horse with a fast walk, he was sound and virtually untirable. His trot was somewhat on the rough side, but it suited Lee, who sat to it rather than posting (rising) in the present-day style. Lee considered Traveller the perfect campaign horse—gentle, easy, comfortable, always ready to move out and never needing to be urged. Traveller has been described as a "one-man horse," for not everyone who had the privilege of riding him agreed with the General that his big grey was an easy ride. One such dissident was his oldest son, Captain Robert E. Lee, Jr., who wrote, "Traveller would not walk a step. He took a short, high trot—a buck-trot as compared with a buck-jump—and kept it up to Fredericksburg, some thirty miles. Though young, strong and tough, I was glad when the journey ended. This was my first introduction to cavalry service. I think I am safe in saying that I could have walked the distance with much less discomfort and fatigue." Since General Lee would not have ridden on active duty any horse with the characteristics described by his son, we can only conclude that the general had what is known as "good hands" and that Lee junior was a somewhat less adept horseman.

The reverence with which General Lee was regarded by his soldiers is well known; probably no other commander in history has been so respected for his qualities as a human being. An especially poignant incident occurred near Chancellorsville where, during exceptionally bloody fighting, the Federals pierced the Confederate position and Lee ordered a counterattack. The battle-weary, exhausted men were reluctant to go back to what many of them regarded as certain destruction, and their officers gathered around Lee in an attempt to dissuade him. Soon a number of private soldiers, having recognized Traveller from a distance and knowing that General Lee must be his rider, gathered in the vicinity. Some of them overheard Lee's insistence upon the attack as well as the officers' disinclination to pursue it, to which Lee finally replied that he personally would lead the attack. As he moved forward toward the battlefront, a shout went up from the men, "General Lee to the rear," and the nearest soldiers grasped Traveller's bridle to prevent the general from going forward. Lee thanked the men for their regard for his personal safety and stated that the attack was so crucial to the Confederate cause, that he intended to launch it with whatever men were willing to follow him. The erstwhile reluctant soldiers, unwilling to expose their beloved leader to danger, then volunteered to resume the attack—but only when Lee had gone to the rear. Traveller was turned around and led some distance away from the battle site before the soldiers released him. The inspired regiment then formed up and moved out as promised to resume the bitter action.

Traveller carried Lee everywhere throughout the war, all the way to the heartbreaking surrender to Grant at Appomattox. After the surrender, Lee mounted his favorite for a ride among the troops to bid his men farewell. Everywhere along the road the big grey was spotted by tired, despairing men lying in the fields, and the shout would go up "here comes General Lee," after which the men would throng into the road to reassure the General that he had fought the good fight, and to listen to his words of counsel. At one point during the journey, he came upon Union General George Meade, whom he had known well in the old army and who had been his opponent at Gettysburg. Meade saluted, and Lee responded with a noncommittal nod. Meade thereupon said, "General Lee, you didn't recognize me, I'm George Meade." Lee took another look and replied, "George, I'm sorry. I didn't know you because of your grey hair. When did you turn grey?" Meade's answer was, "General, you gave me every one of them!"

His parting with his men completed, Lee rode Traveller to Richmond to be reunited with his wife and children. Shortly thereafter, he was offered the presidency of Washington College—renamed Washington and Lee after he accepted the post. Lee rode Traveller the hundred miles from Richmond to Lexington, the site of Washington and Lee, stopping four nights at the homes of old friends. Mrs. Lee was a semi-invalid and the Lexington climate was unsuited to her delicate health. Consequently she was settled at Blue Sulphur Springs, some eleven miles away. Lee virtually "commuted" between Lexington and the Springs, riding his faithful Traveller.

Little by little, the strains of the wearisome war had sapped the energies of both the General and his old war horse. Lee finally succumbed to a heart attack in the fall of 1870. Traveller was shortly to follow his master; soon after Lee's funeral the old war horse developed lockjaw as a result of stepping on a rusty nail. There being no cure, he was mercifully shot to prevent further suffering.

VII
Rienzi

*Sheridan's
Stouthearted Campaigner*

I n September 1861, while his classmates were making headlines with their battlefield exploits, a West Pointer, Philip H. "Fighting Phil" Sheridan was routinely promoted to the rank of Captain and assigned as Quartermaster of the Army of Southwest Missouri, near Springfield. This grand-sounding title merely meant that Sheridan's duties were to scout the countryside looking for horses and mules to buy for the Union forces stationed in the area—one of the lowliest possible assignments for a West Pointer in wartime. As it turned out, Sheridan's impatience with the red tape of this duty resulted in his being given the opportunity to show his worth as a battlefield leader of cavalry—and to make his horse a national celebrity.

In the spring of that same year, when the Civil War was in its infancy, Sheridan held the dubious distinction of being the lieutenant with the longest service in that rank. All of his classmates as well as many lower classmen had moved far up the promotion ladder as the army expanded to meet its wartime need for manpower. Sheridan had been passed over for promotion several times since graduation nine years earlier because his commanding officers considered him to be hot-tempered, rebellious and lacking in cooperation. He was a troublemaker, they said, impatient with routine garrison life and lacking in respect for his superior officers—a "lone wolf" rather than a team player.

This reputation was certainly well deserved, for as far back as his cadet days Sheridan had frequently been in hot water. In his senior year he had received a rebuke from Cadet Sergeant W.R. Terrill and in return attacked him with a bayonet—an action for which he was punished by being "turned back" a year to graduate with the following class. Now, less than ten years later, Terrill was a brigadier general. Even after Sheridan was promoted to the rank of captain, prospects for wartime fame, glory and promotion seemd far out of reach.

In his new post as quartermaster, Sheridan soon discovered that his assistant was a thief, the head of a gang that stole horses from the local farmers, forged bills of sale, sold the stolen horses to the army and pocketed the payments. Sheridan promptly had the assistant brought to trial and became impatient with the delays that the defense counsel managed to bring about. He complained so emphatically and frequently that he became a nuisance to his commanding general, who relieved him and sent him to higher headquarters for reassignment. Sheridan departed to report to General Henry W. Halleck, the Union commander west of the Mississippi.

As it happened, General Halleck had a problem at that time: the new volunteer Second Michigan Cavalry was without a commanding officer and none of the other officers of the regiment had any active duty experience. On the afternoon Sheridan reported for reassignment it had just been brought to Halleck's attention that there was no qualified officer available to take command of the regiment, which had been ordered to set off on a week's raid behind Confederate lines the next morning. At his wits' end, Halleck decided to take a chance and send Sheridan—the only regular officer available—to take temporary command, cautioning him not to be too impetuous.

Independent command was exactly suited to Sheridan's nature, and the qualities of impatience and combativeness which had hampered his career in the peacetime army proved to be just what the cavalry needed in wartime. When the Second Michigan returned from its raid it was obvious that the new commander had made soldiers out of his green troopers. Morale and discipline (which always go hand in hand) were of a high order, and the "on-the-job" training under Sheridan's tireless leadership had paid off handsomely in the many skirmishes behind the lines in which the regiment had been engaged. Sheridan was rewarded by being given permanent command of the regiment and jumped in rank from captain to colonel. Within a month he was a brigadier general, commanding two regiments.

Sheridan started the raid with the Second Michigan on a borrowed horse, far too gentle and pokey for his requirements. One of his troop commanders, Captain Archibald Campbell, had a big, strong Morgan gelding—a handful for an inexperienced rider. Campbell was not much of a horseman and readily admitted to being somewhat afraid of his mount finding him difficult to control. Noting Sheridan's displeasure with his quiet old hack, Campbell offered him the Morgan and Sheridan accepted, naming the horse Rienzi for the Mississippi town that was the objective of the raid. Thus began a partnership of horse and man which was to make them both famous— Sheridan as the preeminent cavalryman of the Union army and Rienzi as the army's best-known horse.

At the time this happy partnership began, Rienzi was a three-year-old, already grown to sixteen hands (very tall for a young horse, and especially so for a Morgan). He was black except for three white ankles, very well built and had a natural fast walk of five miles an hour. Inasmuch as Sheridan was a small man—almost jockey-size—the combination made Rienzi appear even taller than he really was; he was regarded as a giant of a horse by men who saw horse and rider at a distance. The two were inseparable during the four years of combat that followed. Sheridan rode Rienzi continuously in every battle and campaign and wrote in his memoirs that the big black

"never once fatigued despite long marches and short rations." As a battlefield leader, Sheridan was frequently under fire at close range; miraculously he was never wounded, but Rienzi was not that lucky, being wounded "several times." (Sheridan lost exact count, but it is believed that Rienzi took at least five bullets.)

From the beginning, the war went very well for the Union in the West (where Sheridan was commanding the cavalry) and badly in the East (where Robert E. Lee was plaguing a succession of Union commanders). Finally President Lincoln called on General Ulysses S. Grant, who had succeeded Halleck and had earned a reputation as the best Union general, to come East and assume overall command of the Union army. One of Grant's first actions after assuming this new and exalted position was to send for Sheridan and place him in command of all cavalry forces in the East.

Up to this point the Confederate cavalry, under superb leaders such as Jeb Stuart and Wade Hampton, had been having things pretty much its own way. Unlike the Southern cavalry, the Union horsemen had been dispersed as messengers and train guards on security duty rather than being organized into hard-riding assault troops. Sheridan quickly changed this waste of horseflesh, forming his cavalry units into well-disciplined combat organizations, and sent them out to meet the Confederates wherever they could find them. The combination of Grant and Sheridan, two superb leaders of men, marked the beginning of the end for the Confederacy.

Both armies were soon to learn the caliber of the new commander and his black horse. Grant decided that the war could be shortened by a devastating raid on the Shenandoah Valley, the "bread basket" of Virginia, and ordered Sheridan to command the campaign. The Confederates, under famed General Jubal Early, strongly defended the valley, and the opposing forces found themselves stalemated at Cedar Creek, about eleven miles from Winchester. Both sides were holding defensive positions, awaiting reinforcements and supplies, and catching their breath. Secretary of War Stanton ordered Sheridan to Washington for consultation and planning; Sheridan rode over to Martinsburg, the nearest railhead, loaded Rienzi in a boxcar and traveled to Washington for the meeting.

When the meeting ended, Sheridan was impatient to return to his troops. A special train was ordered to take him and Rienzi back to Martinsburg together with two engineer officers who were to survey the defenses at Cedar Creek. One of the engineers, a Colonel Alexander, was enormously fat and not accustomed to riding; consequently the party moved slowly after leaving the train and got only as far as Winchester, where they stayed that night in a private home.

The next morning at breakfast, gunfire was heard from the direction of Cedar Creek. Sheridan called for Rienzi to be saddled. Leaving the others to follow, he took off at a steady trot toward the sound of the action. He soon ran into a large number of panicked Union soldiers fleeing to the rear and learned that foxy old Jubal Early had taken advantage of the Union commander's absence to launch a surprise attack, which had been highly successful. The Union forces, except for a few pockets of determined cavalry, were in full rout and Sheridan faced disaster.

Sheridan rallied the fleeing men, turning them around toward the battle, and then spurred Rienzi forward in a full gallop toward the firing. The road was blocked in many places with groups of disorganized men, Sheridan forced Rienzi to dodge them, often taking to the fields and jumping fences while shouting encouragement to the frightened soldiers. The familiar sight of their beloved leader and his black charger reassured many of those who had campaigned with them in other battles; they began to feel ashamed of themselves and turned back to resume the fight. The reversal became contagious and soon almost all of the unwounded men, inspired by Sheridan on his galloping horse, began to retrace their steps. The sight of their leader racing toward the battle, waving his saber while riding at breakneck speed appealed to their pride as soldiers, and they turned to follow him. The strain on Rienzi was great, for Sheridan was alternately asking him for extended speed and then pulling him to an abrupt halt, in order to give encouragement to his dispirited men. Although the distance between Winchester and Cedar Creek is only eleven miles, it is probable that Rienzi galloped full tilt at least twice that distance as Sheridan ranged back and forth turning his men around.

Three miles below Cedar Creek, Sheridan found his second in command, General Horatio G. Wright, valiantly conducting a delaying action with the few troops that had not panicked. A counterattack to recapture the lost ground was quickly decided on, with Sheridan personally leading it and Wright feeding in the returning troops as they arrived. It must have been thought a lost cause by all but the most stout hearted, for the Confederates were attacking in force and were encouraged at the thought of a quick victory that would rout the Yanks from their homeland. Sheridan's first thought was to rally the troops; he remounted Rienzi, drew his saber and placed his cap on it. Then galloping across the entire front in between the lines, he swung his saber and waved it toward Early's attacking force. Thoughout the battle Sheridan raced Rienzi through curtains of Confederate rifle fire, for all the men in grey recognized the Union general and were doing their best to put him out of action by bringing his horse down.

Sheridan's men—both those who had stayed and those who returned—responded to his courage. As he turned Rienzi directly toward the Confederate line, Sheridan charged forward with a momentum that carried his soldiers all the way back to Cedar Creek whence they had been so ignominiously driven a few hours before. The battle now became a disaster for the Confederates; Sheridan and Rienzi had turned the tide, and Early's men were swept along. Those not taken prisoner fled the area, and the Union's victory was complete. The turn of events so shattered Confederate morale that Sheridan conquered the rest of the Shenandoah Valley in a few weeks' time, and its resources were thereafter not available to the needy Southerners. Grant's strategy had been right. Capturing the Shenandoah did hasten the war's end by denying farm produce to Lee's army. The entire country realized that Sheridan's leadership had saved the day and that it would have been impossible—all would have been lost—had he been mounted on a lesser horse than the gallant Rienzi.

The memorable ride was commemorated in a famous poem, ''Sheridan's Ride,'' by Thomas

Buchanan Read. It was familiar to every schoolboy for generations thereafter until Sputnik and science crowded all but the skeleton of American history from the classroom. Read's lines give equal credit to horse and man, although they somewhat exaggerated the distance Rienzi galloped:

> Here is the steed that saved the day
> By carrying Sheridan into the fight
> From Winchester, twenty miles away.

A writer for *Leslie's Weekly,* a leading periodical of the day, thought that Rienzi was not a glamorous enough name for such a famous horse and decided to call the big black Winchester. The name caught on with the general public (but not with Sheridan or his army) and is the name most commonly used by modern historians in writing about Cedar Creek.

Rienzi continued to be Sheridan's first mount during the rest of the hostilities and carried him all the way through the bitter fighting that culminated in Lee's surrender at Appomattox. It was there that Sheridan's cavalry blocked the retreat from Richmond and forced Lee to ask for terms from Grant. The big Morgan, having more than earned an honorable retirement, was then turned out to pasture in the daytime and bedded down comfortably in a box stall at night, receiving the best of care and enjoying the visits of the curious, who came to see the famous veteran of Sheridan's campaigns. He lived on until 1878, always a center of attraction. When he died peacefully in his twentieth year, it was decided to preserve him by taxidermy and exhibit him at the Smithsonian Institution in Washington, where he is seen by thousands of interested visitors annually.

VIII
Comanche

*Sole Survivor
of the
Battle of the
Little Big Horn*

George Armstrong Custer was the most flamboyant and reckless cavalry leader the American army has ever known, and his reputation attracted a number of soldiers of fortune from overseas to join the famous Seventh Cavalry Regiment. One of these, Captain Myles Walter Keogh, an extremely tough Irishman, had served as a Papal guard after having been forced to leave Ireland as a result of some bloody fights with British landlords.

One of Custer's innovations in the newly formed Seventh was to mount each troop on similarly colored horses—all bays, browns, blacks, chestnuts or greys. When this was accomplished, there was a leftover assortment of mixed colors which fell to the lot of the junior captain, Keogh, to command. This "I" troop became the butt of many jokes as the ugliest-looking troop of the regiment. Keogh, however, was as flamboyant as Custer, and decided that he would acquire a personal mount of his own, contrasting in color to any other horse in the regiment. After some search, he found a powerful buckskin gelding the color of dull clay, belonging to Custer's brother Tom (also a captain of the Seventh). Keogh bought the horse for ninety dollars, a rather high price for an officer's mount in those days.

The Seventh had been formed to combat the increasing Indian resistance to the white man's incursions on their traditional hunting grounds and, shortly after obtaining his horse, Keogh and his troops were engaged in a skirmish with a raiding party of Comanches. The buckskin was wounded by an arrow in the hindquarters, and when he recovered from the wound, he was given the name Comanche. The horse lived to survive the most crushing defeat ever inflicted on the American cavalry when in 1876 the Seventh was wiped out at the Battle of the Little Big Horn—remembered today as the "Custer Massacre" or "Custer's Last Stand."

General Custer was a fearless and highly respected man even though his commands invariably took higher casualties than other cavalry organizations. He graduated from West Point at the start of the Civil War. Although at the bottom of his class in conduct and academics, he ranked high in equitation and tactics. Two years after graduation, before his twenty-fifth birthday, Custer became a major general as a result of battlefield promotions for gallantry in action. Garrison life made him restless but he thrived in combat, and was destined to gain enduring fame not from victory, but from defeat on the battlefield when he died with every member of the Seventh except the horse, Comanche, at the Battle of the Little Big Horn (the final disastrous encounter named after a river in Dakota Territory which formed part of the battleground).

Earlier in Custer's career his Michigan cavalry had been instrumental in blocking Lee's retreat from Richmond by intercepting him at Appomattox, where the Civil War came to an end. Thereafter the Union army had no use for young generals, and Custer reverted to inactive status. Unhappy with civilian life, he leaped at an offer to take acting command of a newly formed cavalry regiment, the Seventh, as a lieutenant colonel.

Custer joined his regiment at Fort Riley in Kansas Territory, and immediately began whipping the Seventh into shape, infusing his own style of panache and morale. Many of the recruits were drifters—men unable to get along in civilian life who adopted the army as a secure home. A large percentage of them, however, were veterans of the recent Civil War, men who were unable or unwilling to adjust to civilian life. Many of the noncommissioned officers had been captains, majors and even colonels in the Confederate army. By law they were not allowed to be commissioned in the Union army.

As the influx of settlers heading West increased, Indian resistance also increased. Treaties made with the tribesmen were broken regularly by politicians in Washington, and the white man's word was scorned by the Indians as "speaking with a forked tongue." Again and again, in violation of solemn treaties, Indians were moved from their reservations to less desirable land in order to satisfy the demands of new settlers. The story is a sad one and a blot on our country's honor, and the cavalry was caught in the middle. Time after time our soldiers were ordered to suppress Indian uprisings brought about because the Indian Bureau reneged on agreements which it had asked the army's commanders in the field to negotiate with the various tribes. One of the most blatant injustices occurred when gold was discovered in the Dakota Black Hills, an area sacred to the Indians as the home of their ancestors. This land had been guaranteed to them as inviolate by the corrupt Grant administration. When prospectors began entering the Black Hills in search of gold, a major Indian uprising took place. The Seventh Cavalry was among the regiments ordered to quell the hostile forces and guard the gold seekers.

Custer received orders to march from Fort Lincoln, across the river from Bismarck and to join General George Crook's larger force near what is now Rapid City, South Dakota. His instructions clearly stated that he was not to initiate a major engagement prior to the joining of forces, but merely to attempt to drive the Sioux warriors toward the larger American force. Happy to be returning to field operations, Custer marched out of Fort Lincoln with the regimental band at the head of the column playing *Garry Owen*, a rousing Irish drinking song which had been adopted as the Seventh Cavalry's own (it is still the favorite march of today's modern and highly

mechanized army). The troops followed the band in alphabetical order, with Captain Keogh, mounted on Comanche, at the head of his unit, eating the dust of the preceding eight troops.

A few days later came disaster. Impetuous Custer committed the tactical error of dividing his force in the presence of a superior enemy. The Sioux with their allies from other tribes, led by Crazy Horse, Sitting Bull, and several lesser chieftains, overwhelmed the cavalrymen. Within twenty minutes the main body under Custer had been annihilated and the detachment commanded by his subordinate, Major Reno, was under heavy siege in the woods into which they had been forced to flee on foot. Indian squaws and children, as was their custom when seeking revenge on the hated white man, followed their warriors, mutilating and torturing the wounded soldiers; Custer's body miraculously was not touched—perhaps because he was killed near the beginning of the battle and his corpse was not recognized in the pile of bodies.

Four long and thirsty days later, the survivors of Major Reno's detachment were rescued by the arrival of a column sent out by General Terry, who had heard rumors from friendly Indians of a massacre at the Little Big Horn. Hardened troopers became violently sick at the sight of the carnage as they searched the battlefield for possible survivors of Custer's command—a search entirely vain except for the discovery of a buckskin horse caught in a dense thicket with his saddle slipped under his belly and seven arrow wounds distributed over his body. This was Comanche, Captain Keogh's sturdy mount, who had somehow escaped the attention of the battlefield scavengers.

It was decided to save Comanche if it was at all possible. The weakened but stouthearted horse was given first aid treatment and slowly walked fifteen miles to the steamer landing at the junction of the Little and Big Horn Rivers where he was put aboard the stern-wheeler *Far West* in a specially constructed stall equipped with slings to support his tired body. Approximately fifty wounded troopers, survivors from Major Reno's beleaguered detachment, and a handful of men from Captain Benteen's troop who had been similarly cut off and routed, were also placed aboard for the 950-mile trip down the Yellowstone and Missouri Rivers to Bismarck. At Bismarck, Comanche was unloaded from the *Far West* and carted in a wagon to the post stables at Fort Lincoln, where he was again placed in slings for several months until his recovery was complete.

Comanche became an instant celebrity as the sole survivor of Custer's last stand. The ladies of the post were delighted to be seen riding him across the plains and through the streets of Bismarck. Finally the Seventh's new commanding officer, tired of seeing the gallant war horse being so exploited for social purposes, issued an order:

General Order No. 7 Headquarters Seventh United States Cavalry
Fort Abraham Lincoln
Dakota Territory
April 10, 1878

The Commanding Officer of Troop I will provide a special and comfortable stall for the horse Comanche. He will not be ridden by any person whatsoever under any circumstances nor put to any kind of work. On all occasions of ceremony Comanche, saddled, bridled, and led by a mounted trooper of Troop I, will be paraded with the regiment.

Thereafter, Comanche had the run of the post, grazing in the flower gardens, coming and going at will to his box stall piled high with comfortable straw bedding. On paydays he frequented the entrance to the noncommissioned officers' club, where he was rewarded with buckets of beer provided by amused troopers. Although grown fat and sassy as the spoiled darling of the post, Comanche was still a cavalry troop horse and turned out, as per General Order No. 7, for all occasions of ceremony. Furthermore, the Seventh was frequently alerted to put down minor Indian uprisings and Comanche was not left behind, but was led along with the spare horses and accompanied the regiment on all its engagements.

Comanche was indeed an iron horse, having survived the seven wounds of the massacre, the four days of thirst, the misery in the thicket after the battle, the weary return trip to Fort Lincoln, the long recovery period in slings, and the petting and fuss resulting from his status as a celebrity. Apparently all the suffering and attention did not alter his disposition, for he remained amiable and seemingly unaffected by his experience. Comanche's long life after the massacre—he outlived Captain Keogh by thirteen years—was due to the care given him by Troop I's blacksmith, Gustav Korn, who tended on the old horse after General Order No. 7 was issued. In addition to caring for Comanche in the garrison, Sergeant Korn, took charge of him in the field until the faithful trooper was killed in a minor skirmish near the Pine Ridge reservation in one of the last of the Indian engagements. Within a month after Korn's death, Comanche followed him to Fiddler's Green, legendary final resting place of all good cavalrymen.

Comanche's death was noted throughout the country, his obituary appearing in newspapers from coast to coast. There was sentiment for preserving the old campaigner by taxidermy; unfortunately, the Seventh Cavalry's funds were insufficient and the underfinanced War Department was unwilling to authorize any such expenditure out of its limited funds. Finally a group of Kansans in the vicinity of Fort Riley, the Seventh's headquarters, agreed to underwrite the cost of stuffing and mounting Comanche to preserve him for posterity.

When the project was completed and a $400 bill was presented for payment, the Kansans failed to meet the obligation. The embarrassed officers of the Seventh, in order to resolve the contretemps and get the bill paid, finally agreed to let Comanche go on exhibition publicly, rather than at regimental headquarters. In return, the Kansas legislature voted funds to pay the taxidermist, and Comanche is today still on exhibit as an official Kansas attraction at the Museum of Kansas University, Lawrence, Kansas.

IX
Bob Haslam's Mustangs

Pride
of the
Pony Express

WANTED

Young, Skinny, Wiry Fellows. Not over 18.
Must be Expert Riders, Willing to Risk Death Daily.
Orphans Preferred. Wages $25 per week.

This unique advertisement in newspapers of 1860 was answered by several hundred adventurous young men. Sixty of them were selected to form one of the most daring groups of horsemen the world has ever seen—the famous Pony Express, which carried the mail between St. Joseph, Missouri, and San Francisco—1,966 miles in eight days, much of it through hostile Indian country.

Many of the young riders of the Pony Express were to gain fame later in life as noted scouts, hunters or Indian fighters. Perhaps its most famous alumnus was young William F. Cody, who joined at the age of seventeen. Better known today as "Buffalo Bill," or "Wild Bill" Cody, he is remembered principally as a great showman whose cowboy and Indian traveling show delighted crowned heads of Europe, as well as the folks at home. But the accolade as the outstanding rider of the Pony Express rightly belongs to a young man named Robert Haslam—"Pony Bob," as he was called by the newspapers.

These were the days before the telegraph and the intercontinental railroad, and the Pony Express was formed to meet the need for reliable and rapid communication between the two coasts. From the railhead at St. Joseph, a route was laid out with relay stations every twenty-five miles, so that the riders could change to fresh horses frequently and maintain the required speed of ten miles an hour. Weight was of great importance, because it affected the horses' ability to go at speed over a distance; preference therefore was given to small, light young men, many of them still in their teens and weighing little more than a hundred pounds. The weight of the mail was also crucial, and a twenty-pound limit was established as the maximum to be carried in the rider's saddlebag. Letters had to be written on onionskin, and were carried at $5 per half ounce; thus a full saddlebag was worth some $3,200.

Of prime importance were the 500 horses chosen for the Express. The finest in the West were secured at an average price of $200, perhaps five times as much as the average cowpony was worth at that time. Only the best would do for this demanding work; they had to be tough, handy, sure-footed and very fast over a distance of ground. Most of these horses, or "ponies," as they were usually called, were native mustangs, perhaps with a dash of Thoroughbred or Morgan blood in their ancestry. The ponies were distributed among the relay stations; one always ready for an approaching rider to make a flying change from the lathered-up pony he had ridden hard from the previous station. Time was of such importance that there would be no delay whatever in changing horses.

The route from St. Joseph to San Francisco lay across some of the most difficult terrain in the West. Starting on the Great Plains, it traversed the snow-capped Rocky Mountains, the salt flats of Utah, the rugged Sierra Nevada range and finally descended to the Pacific coastal area. Winter and summer, in snow, sleet, rain or broiling sun, the Pony Express was in constant operation twenty-four hours every day. The rugged country over which the riders carried the mail was not the only hazard; shortly after the service was inaugurated, several Indian tribes went on the warpath and raided the relay stations between Salt Lake City and Carson City, Nevada. The warriors, mostly Paiutes and Shoshones, ran off with the station ponies, killed the station managers and generally raised havoc with the operation. The riders and their ponies were frequently in danger, and several were killed or wounded by the Indians. The advertisement for expert riders willing to risk death daily was no exaggeration.

Pony Bob first became known to the public in March, 1861, when he helped to set the speed record between St. Joseph and San Francisco. A special effort was made to carry Lincoln's inaugural address as swiftly as possible to the west coast. The month of March, of course, does not provide the most suitable weather for cross-country riding along the Pony Express route. Gales of cold wind sweep the plains; rivers have to be forded at their iciest; the snow drifts are high in the mountains. March of 1861 was one of the worst months ever, with snow so heavy that a mule train had to be used to keep a narrow lane open through a thirty-foot snowbank. Lincoln's address was carried the 1,966 miles in seven days and seventeen hours, at an average speed of 10.6 miles per hour. Pony Bob's contribution was to gallop 120 miles (changing horses, of course, at the relay stations) in eight hours and ten minutes, for an average of 14.7 miles per hour. His section of the route, known as the "ambush trail," lay from Smith's Creek to Fort Churchill in what is now the state of Nevada; the route was aptly named, for Pony Bob was wounded twice by Indian arrows as he carried Lincoln's address.

By the time of this ride, Pony Bob was already a nationally famous personage, as well known to the youth of that day as astronaut John Glenn was to be to the space age generation a century later. The ride that made him every boy's hero took place in 1860, when the Paiutes were aggressively on the warpath all over Nevada, attacking the white settlers on their ranches and even assaulting larger towns such as Virginia City and Reno. Leaving Virginia City one fall evening as the town was alerted for an Indian attack, Bob rode through the hostile forces to Reed's Station on the Carson River only to find that the stationmaster and all the horses had been run off by the Indians. Because of the Indian trouble, Bob had been unable to approach the stations between Virginia City and Reed's, and had actually ridden his mustang sixty miles instead of the normal twenty-five. Unable to change horses at Reed's he watered his tough little mustang, scrounged up a few handfuls of feed in the abandoned stable, and rode on another fifteen miles to Buckland's Station down the river.

Haslam's ride to Buckland's was mostly at a gallop; he was pursued by Paiutes, and it was a demanding effort on the part of his mustang, who had already covered the sixty miles from Virginia City. The superiority of the grain-fed Pony Express horses over the Indian's grass-fed ponies was clearly demonstrated on this stretch of Pony Bob's ride.

When Pony Bob and his trusty mustang reached Buckland's, seventy-five Indian-infested miles from Virginia City, he was dismayed to find that the relief rider refused to go on because of the Indian danger. The station manager offered Bob a bonus of $50 if he would carry on. Bob accepted. Mounting the reluctant relief rider's fresh mustang, Pony Bob took off on a dangerous thirty-five-mile ride along the Carson. Then he pushed on through alkali bottom and sand hills for another thirty miles on the same pony—a sixty-five-mile leg through country that was particularly tiring for a horse to negotiate. Twice more he changed horses and arrived at Smith's Creek almost on schedule after a total ride of 185 miles from Virginia City without rest.

Pony Bob slept nine hours at Smith's and then started the return trip to his home station. At Cold Spring, thirty miles from Smith's, he found the stationmaster slaughtered by Indians. Cold Spring had been his last change of horses the day before, and he had missed the Indian attack there by only a few minutes. The Indians had run off with all the horses at Cold Spring, so Bob had no choice but to continue with the same mustang to the next station—thirty-seven miles farther on. Here he changed horses and pushed on to Buckland's, where the station agent was so impressed with his great ride that he raised the bonus to $100. After resting at Buckland's for an hour and a half, Bob saddled up the mustang that had brought him there two days earlier, crossed the mountains and rode on to Virginia City, where the almost unbelievable feat had begun. All in all, this ride of nearly 400 miles was made within a few hours of schedule and with less than twelve hours of rest for Bob. One of his seven mustangs traveled 150 miles, another 104. Thus two of his seven mounts carried him almost two thirds of the entire ride!

The Pony Express provided an exciting, but short-lived, episode in American history. At its inception it served a much-needed requirement for communications to California, which up to then had been at least a month removed from contact with the East. The development of the railroad and the telegraph doomed the Pony Express as a permanent communications link with the West. It was discontinued after sixteen months of operation, during which it traversed a total of 616,000 miles—the equivalent of more than 25 trips around the world. This effort required great endurance and stamina on the part of both man and horse, whose accomplishments in the face of many hazards contributed much to the fact and folklore of the West. The Pony Express was a heroic epic, made possible not only by brave riders such as Bob Haslam, but also by their unsung mustangs who outraced the Indian ponies and made their speedy way over rugged terrain in all kinds of weather.

X
Chief Joseph's Appaloosa

When Hernando Cortez landed in Mexico in 1519, he brought with his invading Spanish fleet eleven stallions and five mares. One of the stallions was a leopard-spotted roan with white stockings. This unusually marked horse, distinguished by its spotted rump, was known in Libya, in Africa, as a Libyan Leopard Horse. Libyan Leopards, although rare, had been imported to many parts of Europe, and it is entirely possible that Cortez' stallion was one of that breed. This is a logical explanation for the existence of spotted-rump horses in America, because there were none before Cortez arrived.

The Cortez horses became the progenitors of the western horse. The Indians stole them from the border missions of the Southwest and drove them across the Great Plains. One tribe of Indians in particular, the Nez Percé,* bartered with the Plains Indians for a band of spotted-rump horses and began to breed them carefully, with the intention of developing a superior type for the Oregon-Idaho territory on which they hunted and traveled. The Palouse River, named by the French fur traders, was a dominant feature of Nez Percé land, and the spotted horses became known by a corruption of the river's name—Appaloosa.

The Appaloosa horse so popular today for trail riding and horse shows is a direct descendant of the Nez Percé band. Good feeding and care have made him larger and rounder than the skinny, wiry, sure-footed Indian pony of a century ago. The pattern of the Appaloosa today is no less remarkable than that of his ancestor, for the Nez Percé wanted individuality just as much as today's owner, both prizing the bizarre markings.

Because of the Nez Percé's attention to breeding a superior Appaloosa, there developed a strong, hardy, tractable and sure-footed animal that was perhaps the best western horse of its time—superior to the average mount of the U. S. Cavalry.

*Although given a French spelling, the tribe is correctly pronounced *nez purse*.

Proof of Appaloosa superiority was amply demonstrated in 1877 when Chief Joseph, a great Nez Percé Sachem, led the United States Cavalry a frustrating chase covering 1,300 miles in four months across Utah, Wyoming and Montana. The saga of Joseph's running fight against the best of the American army is a remarkable demonstration of courage in the face of overwhelming odds. It was made possible only by the hardihood and courage of the Indians' Appaloosa ponies, which time and again outdistanced their pursuers.

As with so many Indian uprisings, the Nez Percé War was the result of our Indian Bureau's hypocrisy and disregard of treaties that the Indians had accepted in good faith. In this instance, the Indian Bureau decided to move the Nez Percé from their homeland—guaranteed to them forever by treaty—to a new and less desirable area with inadequate grazing land and game to be hunted for food. Chief Joseph argued with his fellows that the white man was too powerful to resist and said: "It is better to live in peace than to die at war." The tribal council overruled him and decided to fight for their rights. Chief Joseph loyally went along with the majority decision and shortly emerged, because of his intelligence and strategic skill, as the leader of the warring tribe.

For a while the war went well for the Nez Percé as they outmaneuvered the cavalry on their spotted horses, charging in and out of the canyons and keeping the blue cavalry off balance. But General Oliver Howard, in command of the army forces, called in more and more troops until the Nez Percés finally had to flee to avoid capture. Howard was sympathetic to the Indians' plight, but he also was a sterling soldier who obeyed orders, and his orders were to quell the uprising. Howard was unhappy with criticism from the War Department and the press for not acting quickly enough, and redoubled his efforts. Joseph led the tribe—about 450 warriors, squaws, and 2,000 Appaloosas—across the steep slopes of the Bitter Root Mountains to Montana, the sure-footed spotted ponies climbing where the cavalry's horses could not follow. There followed a brief respite before Howard caught up by a longer but less precipitous route, and the chase was on again.

The pattern was repeated time after time during the next months, with the federal forces—vastly superior to the Nez Percé in every category except horseflesh—catching up, taking high casualties in comparison with the Indians and taking up the pursuit again as the Indians broke off the hopeless fighting and attempted to flee to Canada, where they would be safe. Joseph's problems were immense; he had to fight a rear-guard action against heavy odds, his braves mounted on half-starved ponies. At the same time he had to take care of the women, the aged and the young. There was little food and no time to hunt game. Forage for the Appaloosas was scant, and the tough spotted horses were feeling the effects. Nevertheless the Appaloosas kept the tribe mobile, although the pace slowed. The white troops were amazed at the Indian ponies. It was inconceivable that tired, underfed horses could continue to outperform the U.S. troopers, particularly when the Indians were encumbered with noncombatants while the cavalry was stripped for action.

Finally, in the cold early winter of October 1877, in the Bear Paw Mountains not a hundred

miles from their sought-after Canadian sanctuary, Chief Joseph was surrounded by several regiments that put his camp under rifle and artillery siege. The Second Cavalry staged a raid which stampeded a large part of the Appaloosa herd, and Joseph realized the Nez Percé could fight no more. Mounting his favorite spotted horse, the brave chief rode slowly toward General Howard and made one of the most stirring speeches ever recorded:

> Tell General Howard I know his heart. I am tired of fighting. Our chiefs are killed. The old men are all dead. He who led the young men is dead. It is cold and we have no blankets. The little children are freezing to death. I want to have time to look for my children and see how many of them I can find. Maybe I shall find them among the dead. I am tired. My heart is sick and sad. From where the sun stands I will fight no more forever.

So ended the Nez Percé's heroic retreat, in which Chief Joseph and his braves on their spotted-rump Appaloosas had outmaneuvered our crack cavalry regiments and held them off with a greatly inferior force for almost four months, while the cavalry chased the Indians for almost 1,300 miles.

XI
Midnight

*Champion
Rodeo Bucking Horse*

In any collection of rodeo riders, when the discussion comes around to naming the champ-
ion bucking horse, a number of colorful names will be proposed—Widow Maker, Double
Trouble, Hell's Angel, War Paint, Tragedy and the like. Almost invariably two horses,
Steamboat and Midnight, will be enthusiastically presented, each with a coterie of vocal rooters.
Steamboat's mark of distinction is that he was said to be the finest bucking horse west of the
Rockies; and Midnight rooters claim that their horse had to be the best or a later champion would
never have been named Five Minutes to Midnight.

Certainly Midnight was the most celebrated bucking horse of the thirties, when there was a
proliferation of such horses available to the rodeo circuit. He was a big, powerful, black gelding
rounded up near Alberta, Canada, and was broken for riding without undue difficulty. He then
spent a short time as a schoolteacher's saddle horse before learning that a powerful buck was a
very effective method of escaping hard work under saddle. After passing through several owners
in rapid succession, all of whom he deftly dislodged whenever the spirit moved him, he wound up
on the rodeo circuit, where he quickly became famous as a spirited competitor.

On the great ranches of the old West, many horses were needed to perform the work of
herding cattle. The practice was to replenish the ranch string of horses (or remuda) with periodic
roundups of the wild horses roaming the countryside. The wild bunch would be branded and some
would be retained to be broken to the saddle, while the rest were turned loose to be rounded up
another time. These roundups, where horses were tried out as saddle broncs, were the forerunners
of today's commercial rodeos, at which cowboys compete to see who is the best rider of a bucking
horse.

The band of 16 horses brought to Mexico by Cortez became the foundation of what later
was to be termed the American bronco, or wild horse. The wild horses originally were small—
stunted by a scarcity of feed—and probably not much bigger than ponies. Three centuries later,

infused by the blood of pioneer horses which had been turned loose or had wandered away from the home ranch, many broncos were found to be of good size, and all of them were hardy and full of fight when men attempted to break them for riding or driving purposes.

In rodeo competition, a bucking horse, or "saddle bronc," has ten seconds to unseat his rider, and the rider is scored on the difficulty of the ride—the tougher the horse, the higher the points for a successful ride. Consequently, the better a horse bucks, the more he is in demand as a mount. The horse is not scored for meanness, but rather for honest performance—a high leap, followed by a jolting landing on the forefeet and a high, back leg kick. To encourage this art form, a bucking strap is tightened under the belly of the horse just forward of the hind legs. Meanwhile the rider must rake his mount's shoulders at each leap with dull spurs, hold the halter shank (the bronco is saddled but not bridled) with one hand and avoid holding on to the saddle with the free hand.

Of the two famous bucking horses, in the opinion of experts, though Steamboat was a very accomplished bucker, the accolade must go to Midnight on the basis of his record. Those who saw both horses in action agree that Midnight threw many more first-class riders and competed much longer than Steamboat. He demonstrated the highest hind leg kick ever seen and invariably made champions of those few riders who managed to stay aboard him for the full ten seconds. In several rodeo saddle bronc competitions, the top award went to the rider who had not lasted the full ten seconds on Midnight in preference to other riders who had stayed the required time on lesser buckers. Midnight is reputed to be the inspiration for the familiar Western slogan—"Thar ain't no hoss that can't be rode and thar ain't no man that can't be throwed." Midnight came very close to being the exceptional "hoss that couldn't be rode." Several factors contributed to Midnight's greatness, including his size (1,400 pounds—very heavy for an active horse), strength and what a fox-hunting man might euphemistically term his "way of going"—a straight-ahead, jarring, high leap followed by an almost perpendicular landing on the forefeet, timed with a hind leg kick directed at the heavens. He was in no sense a tricky bucker—not a wheeler, sunfisher, biter or roller. He defeated his rider honestly, by overpowering him. He was the undisputed champion bucker of his time and the most sought after by riders looking for championship status. When he finally died, after a long career of unseating riders at all the leading rodeos throughout the nation, several hundred cowboys attended a memorial service held to honor the greatest bucking horse of all time. Most of those present had been thrown by the great horse and many of them had been badly injured, but they admired him for his great heart, honest performance and the fame which riding him had brought to those few who had managed a precarious ten-second ride on his strong back.

XII
Jenny Camp

*The Army's
Olympic Mare*

The most demanding test of a horse's ability is the Three Day Event, a combination of dressage, cross-country riding and stadium jumping. This event can be a severe test of a horse's courage, stamina, endurance and disposition, particularly under the stress of international competition. When the nations were oriented to horse cavalry before World War II, the Three Day was known as the all-around military equestrian championship. Today civilian riders dominate the events in many countries, but the performances are still first rate and the competition as intense as when cavalrymen, with almost unlimited reserves of horseflesh to draw on, devoted years of preparation to winning glory for their nations.

In 1936, an Olympic year, the United States Army team was a heavy favorite to win the Three Day event at Berlin. The team's best mount, Jenny Camp, had placed second in the 1932 Olympics under Captain Earl F. Thompson, who was back in the saddle again with her for the 1936 contest. Jenny Camp was an army-bred mare standing 16.1 hands, foaled in 1926—a three-quarters Thoroughbred by the army's premium jumping sire, Gordon Russell, and out of a half-Thoroughbred mare. She was an exceptionally fine Three Day horse at the peak of condition. Other American cavalrymen on the 1936 team were Captain Carl Raguse, a promising younger rider on Trailolka, and Captain John M. Willems, an experienced veteran, on Slippery Slim.

The three days of this international competition are divided according to events. On the first day dressage, the least interesting phase for most onlookers, is featured. The purpose of dressage is to demonstrate how well schooled the horse is in executing various movements—actually basic schooling carried to a high level with the horse quiet, relaxed, supple and highly responsive to his rider's almost invisible application of the aids. Not only is dressage a test of a horse's movement but it also demands alertness and obedience.

On the second day comes the endurance phase, the test of a horse's heart, condition and jumping ability over some of the most horrifying-looking obstacles the mind of man can devise.

XIII
Snowman
Rags-to-Riches Show Jumper

Harry deLeyer was late in arriving at the auction that morning. He had hoped to pick out a quiet beginner's hack for his string at New York's exclusive Knox School for Girls at St. James, Long Island, where he was riding master, but when he arrived he found that a butcher had bought all the horses that were left over from the auction. Nobody had bid for them and the butcher had them loaded on his truck to go to the slaughterhouse to be turned into dog food.

By chance, Harry glanced at the truck and liked the eye of a grey horse whose head was poked over the side. He asked to see the grey, and the butcher somewhat reluctantly off-loaded the horse for inspection. He wasn't much to look at—dirty coat, very thin and haggard, with harness marks worn into his flanks, and in an underfed and overworked condition. But there was something about the look in the horse's eye that appealed to Harry. He offered fifty dollars, which the butcher promptly accepted because it was more than twice what he would have received for the horse at the abattoir.

Who could have guessed that the tired, overworked grey being led from the butcher's truck on that fall morning in 1954 would become one of the world's great show jumpers?

When Germany's Panzer columns invaded Holland during World War II, they overran the farm on which young Harry deLeyer lived, and many of the horses used to work the fields were confiscated for use in pulling the conquering army's supply wagons. Young deLeyer was heartbroken at the loss of the horses. They were his pride and joy and his father had entrusted him with responsibility for their care.

Most farmers in Europe used their horses for pulling wagons, and drove them either from a seat on the wagon or by walking alongside. Harry deLeyer always preferred to ride rather than drive, and it was a common sight to see him sitting astride a big draft horse in the fields.

The long German occupation changed the deLeyer family fortunes, and it was decided that Harry would leave the country when the war ended. But if he was not to be a farmer in the old country, he was determined to stay with horses and decided to come to the United States to look for work as a professional horseman.

Toward the end of the war, about 1944, a grey foal was born to a plow horse in the Amish country near Lancaster, Pennsylvania. The Amish are a fundamentalist religious sect and have rejected many of the conveniences of modern civilization. They prefer the horse and buggy to the automobile, and some of their habits are reminiscent of the customs of late-nineteenth-century America. Their horses are used for farm work rather than sport, and it is likely that the grey colt's owner never expected he had anything other than a plow horse. The colt was just a run-of-the-mill looking youngster with good solid bone, but a little undersized for heavy work.

In 1947, when the colt was a three-year-old, he was broken to harness. At about the same time, Harry deLeyer sailed from Holland to America and found a job working with horses in North Carolina. While Harry was slowly making a name for himself as a top-flight horseman with hunters and jumpers, the grey horse was harnessed to a plow, pulling heavy wagons, being worked strenuously, and apparently not receiving very good care.

As Harry's reputation grew, he moved first to Virginia and then to Long Island, where he became riding master at a boarding school which had long featured first-class riding programs. When Harry went to Pennsylvania to look for some horses to add to the Knox School's string he wasn't looking for jumpers or hunters—horses with animation, presence or good conformation; he would not have gone to the Amish country looking for these. He was hoping on this trip to pick up one or two useful, gentle, all-purpose hacks for the younger beginners to learn on, and decided to attend an auction near Lancaster to see if there might be a bargain horse to fill his requirements. At the same time, the farmer-owner of the grey horse, turned ten years old and presumably past his prime, decided to send him to the auction because he was not big and strong enough to do the heavy farm work.

Now the grey horse belonged to Harry deLeyer. For another twenty dollars the butcher agreed to deliver the animal to the Knox School, where good care and proper feed would slowly bring him into healthy condition. Harry's pupils decided to name the horse Snowman, and he became quite a pet of the younger children because of his gentleness. They climbed all over his back and between his legs and learned to ride on him with complete confidence as he walked or slowly trotted around the ring. He was still regarded as just another useful hack, safe for beginners but not of interest to advanced riders.

After Snowman had been in Harry's string at Knox for about a year, earning his keep as a beginner's horse, a local doctor who was looking for a quiet hack offered to buy Snowman. At that moment Harry had more horses than he needed, and so the sale was made. That night Harry had a call from the doctor, who said that Snowman had jumped a four-foot fence and run away. He didn't go too far that night—just back to the school where he jumped into the paddock, a performance that was repeated several times until the good doctor became exasperated and asked Harry to buy the horse back.

Needless to say, Harry deLeyer was delighted to have Snowman back again, because he now knew that the horse had a jumping potential which nobody had recognized. Never having been schooled at a jump, Snowman was very green, but he had a natural spring and balance, which when combined with his placid disposition gave a hint of future greatness over fences. On the debit side, Snowman was somewhat of a heavy goer at the gallop, his plow-horse ancestry not contributing much to a free-moving gait. He was on the small side (less than sixteen hands, a hand being four inches) for a jumper, and his age—going on twelve—was definitely against him. Most jumpers have passed their peak after seven or eight. Harry debated the wisdom of schooling Snowman for jumping; it would take much time and his period of usefulness would be relatively short. Perhaps his affection for the tranquil old horse outweighed the more practical arguments. At any rate, he decided to make a jumper out of Snowman and to see just how good a competitive show horse he might become.

Harry brought Snowman along slowly and thoroughly, resisting the temptation to "make him in a hurry" without giving him a solid foundation. Many hours of slow work over low fences, with gradually increasing heights as the horse developed confidence, were spent patiently in the ring after the regular horsemanship classes had been completed for the day. As Snowman's style improved, more difficult jumps were taken, and the distances between them were varied. A horse can learn to jump a single fence rather quickly, but jumping a course comprising eight to twelve difficult fences, some high, some wide spread, and with several changes of direction, is a far more difficult matter. Many horses have their dispositions ruined by being asked to jump a difficult course before they have had sufficient experience. They become panicky and either rush their jumps or learn to refuse. Harry knew that Snowman would face top-flight competition on the Long Island and metropolitan New York show circuit at the famous, long-established shows that attract the best horses in the country, and he wanted to make sure that Snowman would be equal to the competition. It was almost two years after Snowman had jumped over the doctor's fence before he was entered in an open jumping class at one of the smaller shows with Harry in the saddle.

Snowman's first year as an open jumper was an unqualified success. He was almost always in the ribbons and quickly became locally famous as the quiet horse with the big, smooth jump. Age had whitened his coat so that he was easy to identify. Nothing seemed to bother him; he took the stiffest Liverpool—a jump composed of a ditch set in front of a high, vertical fence—as easily as a simple brush jump. He delighted in jumping clean, without touching an obstacle, never wasting himself by overjumping. The combination of Snowman's long training and Harry's quiet, but firm seat and aggressive style kept him on the bit and alert on the course. When they had left the arena after a faultless performance and Harry dropped the reins, Snowman would relax and stand patiently as young and old swarmed around to get a closer look at the old campaigner. By the end of the first season it was apparent that Snowman could hold his own with the best open jumpers anywhere in the country; plans were made to go after the Horse of the Year award in the following year, 1958. This award is in effect the national championship and is based on the most points won in shows recognized by the American Horse Shows Association, governing body of the country's horse shows. Campaigning for Horse of the Year means traveling every week to a different show, many of them of four or five days' duration and situated in various parts of the country. Snowman and Harry deLeyer were constantly on the go all during the long season from early May to November. Long van trips, unfamiliar stables, changes of water and feed, and the constant pressures of competition in strange surroundings against horses and riders more familiar with local conditions require a great deal of stamina on the part of both horse and rider. Snowman and deLeyer were more that equal to the situation, piling up a commanding lead of wins as the summer progressed and meeting and beating the best of the opposition wherever they went. By November when the National Horse Show, the circuit's most important event was held at New York's Madison Square Garden, Snowman was uncatchable and had firmly secured Horse of the Year honors. To prove his merit he entered and won the National's championship, beating all the top open jumpers brought there from all sections of the country.

Because the National Horse Show attracts the best horses and a large audience, Snowman's championship there made him an instant celebrity and an object of great interest. He became known as the Cinderella horse—a name applied by an imaginative sportswriter in describing Snowman's humble beginnings. Fan mail began to arrive at the deLeyer stable, some fans asking for wisps of mane or tail or one of Snowman's old shoes. The deLeyers figured out that the requests for tail hair, if fulfilled, would leave Snowman hairless on that extremity. Obviously they were not inclined to inflict such an indignity on the old campaigner; so a polite form letter was devised explaining their inability to provide the requested talismans.

Visitors in increasing numbers began to arrive at the deLeyer stable—Hollandia Farm in St. James, Long Island—asking to see Snowman. Frequently one of the deLeyers would point out a sleepy looking, almost white horse standing in the paddock with perhaps a child twined around his neck, two on his back and one or two playing under his belly. Almost as frequently, the visitors would assume that the deLeyers were playing a game with them and would insist on seeing the real Snowman. It took quite a bit of convincing before doubters were persuaded that the gentle pet was the same horse who performed so boldly over the stiff jumps at the major horse shows.

Although Snowman was justly famous as Horse of the Year and was not getting any younger, he came up to the 1959 season in such fine shape that deLeyer decided to take another shot at Horse of the Year honors—something often attempted and rarely attained twice in succession. Although his margin of victory was somewhat narrower, Snowman managed to win the award decisively in 1959 and was almost everybody's favorite during the season. People who had never before been to a horse show, many of them with little or no knowledge of what it was all about, came to see Snowman in action, and he seldom disappointed them. Again he won the National's championship to thunderous applause, and again the public deluged Hollandia Farm with letters and phone calls. All this attention did not affect Snowman at all. His disposition remained marvelously calm and he was still the neighborhood children's pet.

By this time Harry deLeyer had received many tempting offers to sell his champion jumper, but the two had become so attached to each other that he firmly declined to part with the horse that had been the means by which he had achieved national recognition as a superb rider and trainer. The decision was made easier because Snowman was then in his sixteenth year, and obviously could not go on much longer against younger horses.

For the next two years Snowman was campaigned lightly, with no intention of competing for national honors in the strenuous competition which that goal demanded. Finally he was retired and turned out to pasture at Hollandia Farm where on any sunny day he could be seen surrounded by children.

XIV
Steel Dust

*Legendary
Quarter Horse*

W hat is the world's richest horse race? Where is it held? What breed of horses race in it? Many of us might answer that it is the Kentucky Derby or one of the famous stakes run in New York, Florida or California. Certainly most of us would assume it was for Thoroughbreds, for when we think of racing, we think of a Man o' War, Citation, Seabiscuit, Count Fleet, Nashua, Swaps or Native Dancer—to name only a few famous racers. We would be wrong; the world's richest horse race is held each year on Labor Day at Ruidoso Downs, New Mexico, and the winner's purse is about three times as large as the winner's purse in the Kentucky Derby. In 1972, the winner's share was $295,000 and the total purse was $925,000! What's more, the race is for a breed known as the American Quarter Horse.

Quarter Horses are so called because of their ability to run a quarter of a mile in very fast time. In Colonial times the Virginia gentry liked to race their horses but, this being in the days before oval racetracks, the sport was conducted in lanes cut through the wilderness. Cutting these lanes involved a lot of wearisome labor, so they tended to be on the short side and averaged a quarter-mile in length. Today, Quarter Horses are still raced only that short distance, and the track is a straight path with no turns. There is no crowding for the rail, as in a race with turns, since there is no ground to be saved from the start to the finish wire. The horses run abreast of each other down the track, and unless one is directly on the finish line it is difficult to know the winner, because there is very little difference between horses at short distances; they generally tend to finish only noses apart, much as in the Olympic 100-meter dash for men or women.

Although Janus, a small Thoroughbred imported into Virginia from England in the late eighteenth century, is regarded as the foundation sire of the breed, the popularity of the Quarter Horse today—more Quarter Horses than Thoroughbreds are registered each year—stems largely from a bay stallion foaled in Kentucky and brought to Texas as a yearling in 1844. Steel Dust, as he was called, was by an unknown sire (possibly a Thoroughbred) out of a Thoroughbred mare; he stood a little over 15 hands (five feet) and weighed about 1,200 pounds. Steel Dust soon earned a reputation for speed throughout the countryside now known as Dallas County.

In the Southwest at that time, the mustang was king. For more than three hundred years, these descendants of Cortez's band of Spanish horses had been working cattle, expanding northward from central Mexico. In Texas the cowmen swore by their mustangs as the best in the world, not only for their "cow sense" but for speed and agility. Hence there were many challenges around Dallas to test the local horses against the newcomer, Steel Dust. The mustang rooters backed their opinions with their pocketbooks and learned the hard way that the big bay from Kentucky was the fastest horse they had ever seen. On the theory that "if you can't lick 'em, join 'em," the Dallas cowmen soon became earnest backers of Steel Dust against all comers.

A match race was arranged against a fast horse named Monmouth, whom the cowmen around Sherman and Jefferson in north Texas considered unbeatable. The race was held at McKinney, Texas, in 1855; interest was so high that the court closed for the day. The throng that came to town from the surrounding ranches and neighboring towns was so large that the local hotel, the Foote House, was turned over to the ladies and the men slept wherever they could.

The Dallas cowmen's pockets were bulging with cash after the race, for Steel Dust's victory over Monmouth was decisive, and word soon spread that he was the fastest horse in the West—the one to beat. Consequently, many good mares were bred to him and Steel Dust blood is found today in all of the good modern Quarter Horse families. Not only did he stamp his progeny with speed, but also with the quick turning ability and docile temperament of the ideal cow horse.

Although the Quarter Horse was originally developed for racing, he bears very little resemblance to his ancestor, the Thoroughbred. Whereas the Thoroughbred is lightly built, with long legs and flat muscle, the Quarter Horse stands much "lower to the ground," with thick legs, bunched muscles and a much larger proportion of his weight carried on his front legs. Because he carries so much weight in front, he tires more easily than the Thoroughbred, but this distribution enables him to start faster and turn more quickly. In addition to his racing ability over short distances, the Quarter Horse has the speed, agility and weight to make him an ideal cowboy's mount, particularly for roping and holding cattle.

The ultimate test of a good cow horse is "cutting" ability, a term that refers to cutting out a selected animal from the herd—perhaps a calf from its mother, or a maverick to be branded. Cutting requires high intelligence, catlike agility, quick starting and stopping and a calm disposition. The "Steel Dusts" had these qualities in abundance, and the famous stallion's get from the Texas mustang mares were a distinct improvement over the typical mustang. They were stronger, better balanced and more adept at ranch work, and were soon universally accepted as the best cow horses in the Southwest.

The 1850's and 60's were years of great expansion in the cattle industry, from the Great Plains northward to Canada. This was the era of the great cattle drives from Texas to the railheads of Kansas, and the ranchmen soon found that their small mustangs, which had served so well for so many years on the home ranges, were not as suitable as the Quarter Horses for the long, arduous work on the trail. Thus, the fame of the Quarter Horse spread far and wide, wherever cattlemen congregated, and the breed became greatly in demand not only for racing but for range work. Today the Quarter Horse stands supreme as the working rancher's horse as well as for rodeo work, and the legendary mustang has all but disappeared from the scene. Since 1950, when the American Quarter Horse Association was formed, the line has been improved, tending toward a finer head and less bunched muscles.

Although Steel Dust is the most famous of the Quarter Horse breed—no other Quarter Horse ever having been so much written or talked about—there were several others of note imported to Texas in the last century, contributing to the legends of the West. When Sam Houston was elected president of the Republic of Texas in 1849, one of his first acts was the establishment of a policy to improve the breed of mustang cow horses by an infusion of Quarter Horse blood from the East. Hence, a remarkable eleven-year-old stallion, Copperbottom, was bought in Lancaster, Pennsylvania, and brought to Texas, where he served as a sire around Huntsville and Sulphur Springs for almost two decades. Like Steel Dust, Copperbottom had a strain of Janus blood; he was a grandson of famous Diomed, the greatest racehorse of his time. Thus, Copperbottom's contribution to improving the breed of cow horse was significant, though not as great as Steel Dust's. The two were much of a type, however, and their descendants had similar characteristics of conformation, disposition and agility—all of which helped to establish a breed pattern.

Aside from Steel Dust and Copperbottom, the best-known Quarter Horse of that era was a half-Thoroughbred, Shiloh, foaled in Illinois and brought to Texas in the late 1840's. Like Steel Dust, Shiloh had the thick muscles and heavy front end which distinguish the breed, and he also had a reputation for speed. It was inevitable that a match race should be held to see which of the two champions was in fact the greater. Both horses had many devoted adherents, all willing to back their opinions with substantial bets. The match was scheduled to be held at Dallas in 1855, with twelve-year-old Steel Dust giving away several years to his younger rival. Which of the two was actually faster will never be known, for Steel Dust, impatient to start, reared up in the chute and broke a board which pierced his shoulder. According to some reports he ran in spite of the injury, and won, but it appears more probable that the race was forfeited. However the ultimate tribute to Steel Dust came from Shiloh's owner, Jack Batchler. He so admired his horse's rival that he sent many of his fillies by Shiloh to be bred to Steel Dust, and many of the top Quarter Horses today—on the race track, ranch, or rodeo circuit—are the result of the mingling of these two great bloodlines.

Steel Dust never raced again after the injury. He spent the rest of his fruitful life in the stud on the ranch at Ten Mile Creek near Lancaster, Texas, establishing his reputation as a prepotent sire of Quarter Horses, many of which—a century later—are still known as "Steel Dusts" rather than by the breed name. In fact, should you hear a horseman refer to his mount as a Steel Dust, it is assumed that you understand he means Quarter Horse.

XV
Man o' War
The "Mostest" Racehorse

Scores of names come to mind when one attempts to select the outstanding American racehorse of all time. Surely the renowned Secretariat, Citation, Tom Fool, Swaps, Nashua, Native Dancer, Dr. Fager, Kelso and one or two others would be put forward by those whose familiarity with the racetrack is confined to money winnings in the inflationary post World War II period. But dollar winnings per se do not have much influence on the judgment of the experts; what counts most are the conditions under which a horse raced, the caliber of the opposition faced and beaten and the ability to transmit speed and stamina through breeding to produce winning progeny. Based on these qualifications, one horse—Man o' War—leads the field by a wide margin, in the opinion of an overwhelming majority of horsemen. His greatness is the standard by which aspiring horses are measured, just as home run hitters are compared to baseball's immortal Babe Ruth.

In 1918 the chairman of the Jockey Club, August Belmont, volunteered for army service at the advanced age of sixty-five. He was commissioned a major and stationed in Paris with the American Expeditionary Force. Being preoccupied with his military duties and far removed from the racing scene on the other side of the Atlantic, he decided to consign his entire crop of home-bred yearlings to the sales at Saratoga Springs, New York. Included in the shipment was a big-boned, long-legged chestnut colt which Mrs. Belmont had christened Man o' War, martial names being in vogue for war babies in that patriotic era. Man o' War had been sired by Fair Play, a great racehorse and money winner with a notoriously bad disposition, and was out of a relatively unknown brood mare, Mahubah, who had won only $700 in her racing career but had impeccable blood lines. Top price at the yearling sales that year was $14,000 for a horse long since forgotten; Samuel D. Riddle, of Maryland, bought eleven, including Man o' War, for a mere $5,000.

Back in Maryland, the Glen Riddle trainer, Louis Feustel, soon realized that he had a most unusual and promising colt on his hands. Man o' War's stride was four feet longer than the average; he was tremendously strong and well-muscled and, unlike many Thoroughbreds in

77

training who are finicky eaters, he was always hungry; in fact a snaffle had to be kept in his mouth to prevent him from bolting his food. He liked to run as much as he liked to eat, and his big appetite was helpful in converting oats into muscle and growth.

Some of Fair Play's bad manners were also evident in the son. Man o' War bucked off every exercise boy at the Glen Riddle training track during the course of his schooling; this was due to exuberance, rather than evil disposition. He resented restraint and just wanted to run as soon as a boy was in the saddle. Many hours had to be spent in teaching the big colt (whom the stable hands nicknamed "Big Red," as his golden chestnut coat darkened to a mahogany hue) to be rated, that is, to gallop at whatever speed the rider desires. The ability to be rated is essential for a top-quality racehorse when he is asked to run a distance. Otherwise, he will be burned out and winded after the first half mile or so, and have no reserve speed to call on for the driving finish.

Man o' War's first race as a two-year-old was in 1919 at the Belmont racetrack (named for his breeder's father) in New York. He broke (left the starting gate) last, but caught up with the rest of the field very quickly and was cantering at the finish, six lengths in front of the second horse. Because of his slow start, he was given much schooling at breaking faster, which made him excitable before every subsequent start and caused some unhappiness among the unfortunate assistant starters who had to handle the big, headstrong colt. Later in his career, he once delayed the start of an important race by twelve minutes, fighting the assistant starters who were trying to get him to line up quietly; such effort might well have taken the edge off a lesser horse, but Man o' War could afford the wasted energy and still go to the front, hold and increase his lead and win eased up while the other racers were being driven.

Four days after his first start, Man o' War was back on the track again, winning a short dash by three lengths. Two weeks later at the Jamaica track he won his third race, carrying top weight of 120 pounds; two days later at Aqueduct he won again under 130 pounds—a very high weight which few two-year-olds are asked to assume. Four wins in as many starts in nineteen days was quite a bit of work for a green youngster, and Mr. Riddle began to suspect what the public was already sure of—that he had a potential champion on his hands. It was decided to race Man o' War at Saratoga, where he had been bought as a bargain yearling the summer before. Here the best two-year-olds in the country race every August. Man o' War's first race at the famous old upstate New York track was won handily, as was his next start in the United States Hotel Stakes—a major event of six furlongs (three quarters of a mile). This win established him as a sensational performer and a public idol, and he was invariably the heavy favorite in every race thereafter.

Another important Saratoga race for two-year-olds is the Sanford Memorial, in which Man o' War was established by the bookmakers as the odds-on favorite at 1 to 2, meaning that the bettor must put up $2 to make a profit of $1 if his horse wins. The number of times a two-year-old has been odds-on can probably be counted on the fingers of one hand. The bookmakers' predilection for Man o' War in the Sanford was especially interesting because several other very good two-year-olds—there was a banner crop in that year of 1919—were also entered, including Golden

Brown, owned by Mr. Riddle's niece, Mrs. Walter Jeffords, and a very fast colt named Upset.

As the field reached the starting barrier, an inexperienced assistant starter took Man o' War in hand and roughed him up, an action to which the big colt took vigorous exception. The starter turned him away from the barrier (this was before the day of the starting gate with its individual stalls, now used at all tracks) to lead him away and try again for a straight approach. At that moment the barrier was sprung, and the rest of the field took off, leaving Man o' War at the post. Jockey Johnny Loftus, his rider, took off in what appeared to be a hopeless chase. Man o' War caught up with the next-to-last horse at the end of half a mile. Coming around the turn for home, Loftus attempted to save ground by trying to get through on the rail, for Man o' War was full of run and eager to go to the front. The stratagem failed, however, for Loftus found himself boxed in by Upset in front and Golden Brown on the outside; he had no choice but to pull back and try to go around the field on the outside—the long way home. Man o' War turned on a remarkable burst of speed coming up the homestretch in the middle of the track and passed all the others except the winner, Upset, to whom he had conceded fifteen pounds of weight. Three strides past the finish line, Man o' War's nose was in front, but it was too late; the aptly named Upset—backed by a happy handful of hunch players who had bet him at 100 to 1—had won. Despite this loss—the only defeat of his career—many observers believe that this was Man o' War's greatest race, because of the courage he displayed. In the face of enormous difficulties, he came close to accomplishing the impossible.

Ten days later, in a fairly run race, Man o' War won the Grand Union Hotel Stakes without being extended. Among his victims that day was Upset. Before the Saratoga meeting ended, he won his next two starts, including the Futurity, in those years regarded as the most important of all races for two-year-olds. Man o' War was then sent down to the Maryland farm to unwind and spend the winter growing into three-year-old form. And grow he did. As his huge appetite dictated, he was fed all the hay he could eat plus twelve quarts of oats daily—in four feedings, at 3:30 and 11:30 A.M.; 5:15 and 9:30 P.M.—a substantial diet for a horse not in training.

In 1920, his three-year-old year, Man o' War's first start was in the Preakness at the Pimlico track near Baltimore. His old jockey, Johnny Loftus, who had ridden him in all of his races as a two-year-old, had been suspended from racing for infractions that had nothing to do with his rides on Man o' War. A new rider, Clarence Kummer, was engaged and became Man o' War's regular jockey. Kummer knew the big chestnut well, having been his exercise boy at Saratoga. They won the Preakness in typical Man o' War style, starting with a great burst of speed, taking the lead early and holding it against all challenges and easing up at the finish when the competition was thoroughly outdistanced. Second that day was Upset, beaten decisively. Today the Preakness is known as "the second jewel in the Triple Crown," the other two being the Kentucky Derby and the Belmont Stakes. The question is often asked why Man o' War did not enter the Kentucky Derby two weeks before the Preakness in an attempt to win the three races, emblematic of the championship for three-year-olds. It must be remembered that half a century ago the Triple Crown was not so highly regarded as it is today, and the Kentucky Derby had not yet become an important race capable of attracting the best three-year-olds. Mr. Riddle passed it up as being of not much interest, and so Man o' War's name will not be found on the roster of Triple Crown winners.

Next was the one-mile Withers Stakes, in New York. Taken under restraint by Kummer shortly after the start, Man o' War won galloping and still managed to break the existing world's record for the distance, setting a new record of 1:35 1/5—a full second under the old time. Had he been extended, his time would undoubtedly have been much faster; Kummer was merely trying to win comfortably without asking his horse for any more effort than necessary. Next came the Belmont, in which only one other horse was entered, other eligibles having dropped out, conceding that Man o' War could not be beaten. The other starter, Donnacona, was no match for Man o' War, and Kummer had difficulty in holding his eager mount down to a twenty-length win over the mile-and-three-eighths distance. Astonishingly, in view of the restraint under which Man o' War was held, the time was a new world's record of 2:15 1/5, not broken until 1966 in Australia, and still an American record. The bookmakers sent Man o' War off in the Belmont at prohibitive odds of 1 to 100, to the cheers of "Chicago" O'Brien, an ex-bricklayer turned gambler, who put up $100,000 to get back $101,000.

The Belmont was typical of Man o' War's career as a three-year-old. In 1920, in six of his eleven races, all of which he won, only one other horse appeared to challenge him, so great was his ability. In one race, the Lawrence Realization, all the original entries were scratched when Man o' War was entered. Mrs. Jeffords entered her horse, Hoodwink, as a sporting gesture to give her uncle some sort of race. Kummer was instructed to hold Man o' War back and not make Hoodwink look bad. The jockey did his best, but Man o' War still won by a hundred lengths. In the Stuyvesant Handicap, another two-horse race, Man o' War carried thirty-two pounds more than Yellow Hand, and beat him with ease. And Yellow Hand was the champion four-year-old!

Except in a few weight-for-age races, where the weights are fixed, Man o' War invariably was given more weight to carry than any of his opponents. Handicappers figure that a two-pound difference in weight is equivalent to one length. Thus in the Yellow Hand race, Man o' War was giving his opponent a sixteen-length advantage. Perhaps the best measure of his remarkable ability are the eight world and track records he set as a three-year-old while carrying top weight. Only once in that year was Man o' War really extended, in what is still often recalled as the greatest race ever run, the Dwyer Stakes at Aqueduct. Another truly great horse, John P. Grier, had been carefully prepared to meet Man o' War, and was extremely fit on the day of the race, whereas Man o' War had been in a long, tiring campaign. In this, another two-horse race, Man o' War carried 126 pounds and John P. Grier carried 108, a difference of eighteen pounds, or a handicapper's nine lengths. The two ran neck and neck, stride for stride, both breaking the world's record for 6½ furlongs in 1:19 3/5 and tying the record for the mile (1:35 1/5), which Man o' War had set as a two-year-old. They still had an eighth of a mile to go when John P. Grier got a nose out front.

Jockey Kummer touched Man o' War once lightly with the whip, and "Big Red" surged ahead to win going away by one-and-a-half lengths.

Man o' War's last race was a match against a champion older horse, Sir Barton, the first winner of the Triple Crown. The race was for a winner-take-all $7,500. (This may seem like peanuts today, but it was important money a half-century ago when the Preakness purse, for example, was less than $6,000—not even a tenth of its present value.) In a workout the day before, the big chestnut was timed in 20 2/5 seconds for the quarter mile, faster than any horse had ever been known to do it. The next day Man o' War beat Sir Barton by seventeen lengths, lowering the track record for a mile and a quarter by 6 2/5 seconds.

In his two-year racing career, Man o' War beat the best fifty horses of his age or older, losing only once by a whisker as a result of atrocious handling. His racing record was superb, with twenty wins in twenty-one starts, and his earnings of $250,000 were a record at that time. He had won carrying as much as 138 pounds and giving away as many as 30. Three times he had started at odds of 1 to 100. He held eleven records, some of which endured for more than thirty years despite the fact that he was almost never asked to extend himself. He was retired only because the handicappers had announced that, should he return to the track as a four-year-old, they would be obliged to give him weight imposts of 140 pounds or more—the heaviest weight in modern racing history. Obviously, the handicappers were going to keep piling weight on Man o' War until he was beaten by some lesser horse, and Mr. Riddle had no desire to subject his champion to that kind of indignity. So the big chestnut champion, the "mostest horse" ever to race (in the words of his faithful groom, Will Harbut) was sent to stud in Kentucky for the final test of greatness—the ability to beget great horses. The stud fee was set at $5,000, an unheard-of sum in those days when $500 was the top breeding price, with many good stallions standing for as little as $50.

The big proud horse remained active in the stud for more than twenty years, with highly successful results. More than 80 per cent of his progeny started at the track, a very high ratio compared with the average. Mr. Riddle gave Man o' War only limited opportunity with outside mares, preferring to reserve his services for his own brood mare band, which was not of top quality. As a consequence, Man o' War was not available to many of the outstanding and proven brood mares, which would have assured his siring foals of premium quality. In view of these limitations, the record of his progeny becomes even more impressive: two of his sons won the Kentucky Derby and one of them, War Admiral, won the Triple Crown. Battleship won the Grand National steeplechase, and Blockade was three times winner of the Maryland Hunt Cup. The Man o' War bloodline a half-century later is still sought by breeders and is prominent in flat racing, steeplechasing, the hunt meets and the horse show ring. Man o' War met the ultimate test of a good sire, prepotency, or the ability to pass on his great qualities of speed, endurance and conformation to his get even when the mare was of lesser quality.

In his years in the stud, Man o' War sired 379 foals that won almost 1,300 races. And he outlived almost all of them, dying in November 1947. Truly he was the greatest of the great.

XVI
Battleship

Winner
of the
Grand National

The world's most famous race over obstacles, and certainly the most demanding test of horse and rider, is the Grand National at Aintree, England. First run in 1839 and held continuously over the same course ever since, except for a handful of wartime years, this annual classic consists of thirty awesome fences presented on a triangular course of four miles, 856 yards. Its distance calls for both endurance and sprinting ability; many horses have one or the other quality, but few have both. The high, stiff fences require superior jumping ability and agility, and the sharp turns penalize a horse that is not extremely responsive to his rider's aids. Ability alone is no guarantee of finishing the race, for racing luck is necessary to avoid the fallen and riderless horses which sprinkle the landscape from the first fence onwards; observers agree that the safest place to be is in the lead, where one has only his own mount to worry about.

Fortunes have been spent in the attempt to win the Grand National, particularly by Americans, and the results have almost always been disappointing to foreign entries. Rubio, in 1908, was the first American-bred horse to win; he was foaled in California, but was owned by an Englishman during his racing career. In 1923, the winner was Sgt. Murphy, owned by an American student at Cambridge, Stephen (Laddie) Sanford, whose father had bought the horse as a hunter for his son from an English farmer. When Sgt. Murphy proved to be too hot in the hunting field for young Sanford, he was put to steeplechasing. The next American victory was by Jack Horner, a horse A. C. Schwartz bought just a month before the race with the express intention of purchasing a winner. In 1933, Kellsboro Jack, an Irish-bred horse bought by F. Ambrose Clark and sold by him to his wife for one pound sterling, was the winner. None of these could be considered wholly American from the standpoint of having been bred, schooled and owned completely in American hands. The first such genuinely all-American entry was Battleship, a son of Man o' War, who in 1938 carried the colors of Mrs. Marion du Pont Scott of Virginia, to beat a strong field of thirty-eight other fencers.

Battleship was a small horse as steeplechasers go, standing only 15.2 hands, and was actually the smallest horse to win since 1871. He also had the distinction of being one of the few stallions ever to win the big event, and his rider, seventeen-year-old Bruce Hobbs, was the youngest jockey ever to ride a Grand National winner. The pair was regarded as somewhat of a curiosity rather than a serious contender, and their chances were considered so slim that the usually knowledgeable English bookmakers, or "turf accountants," to their ultimate sorrow sent them off at odds of 40 to 1. Had the British bettors done their homework a little more carefully, their regard for Battleship might not have been so casual, for Mrs. Scott was an extraordinarily successful breeder of good steeplechasers and the Man o' War bloodline is noted for speed, endurance and jumping ability. Furthermore, Battleship's racing career in America was remarkable; he had been a stakes winner in flat racing before being converted to steeplechasing. Always raced on big tracks against quality opponents, he was the outstanding American champion over fences and was in prime condition. The "little horse with the big heart" was a much more serious contender than the odds indicated.

Almost all the fences are considered dangerous, most being five feet high on the takeoff side and as much as three feet lower at landing. Thus an inexperienced or tired horse tends to overjump and come down in a somersaulting fall. Many of the obstacles are made more difficult by ditches, both deep and wide, some on the takeoff side and others hidden on the landing side. The first fence, only forty feet wide, is much too narrow to accommodate all the eager starters anxious to get to the front, and invariably some horses fall there in the "cavalry charge" to avoid the traffic jam. Becher's Brook is a thick thorn fence with a fearsome three-foot drop on the landing side, which also contains a wide ditch six feet deep; a fall into the ditch is almost equivalent to falling off a two-story roof. Valentine's Brook is a near duplicate of dreaded Becher's. Canal Turn is a five-foot wall with a six-foot ditch on the takeoff side which, immediately after being jumped, requires a quick right-angle turn to avoid falling into the canal just ahead (which some out-of-hand horses have done in spite of their riders' best efforts to avoid this disaster). The Chair is the highest, widest and narrowest obstacle of all, with a six-foot ditch at takeoff. The fifteen-foot water jump has a two-and-a-half-foot fence on the approach side.

Some idea of the chaos which often occurs during the running of a Grand National is illustrated by the performance of two entries in the 1928 race—Easter Hero and American-owned Billy Barton: Easter Hero stuck momentarily on top of the Canal Turn fence and Billy Barton had to jump not only the fence by also the struggling Easter Hero—a remarkable acrobatic feat. Easter Hero then wriggled off the fence and fell into the ditch on the takeoff side. He scrambled to his feet and ran up and down the length of the ditch trying to find a way out. Some twenty following horses refused to jump Canal Turn because of frantic Easter Hero's interference, and had to withdraw. Meanwhile Billy Barton raced on, catching up with the leader, Tipperary Tim, at the last fence. A riderless horse which had kept company with Tipperary Tim up to this point swerved into Billy Barton and interfered with his landing so that he fell just as victory appeared certain, for Billy Barton was running much faster than the tiring leader. Jockey Cullinan was unhurt and had managed to hold on to the reins; he remounted Billy Barton in a flash and took off after Tipperary Tim but was unable to close the gap before the finish line. Tipperary Tim was the only horse in the race not to fall or refuse, and Billy Barton was the only other to finish—out of a starting field of forty-two in that year's Grand National.

There are no post positions or starting gates at Aintree. The nervous field mills about at the starting line waiting for the signal. As the flag was dropped, the 1938 favorite, Royal Danieli, a powerfully built gelding who dwarfed the American entry, took off confidently to assume the lead. Battleship, submerged in the ruck, gradually worked his way forward to take second position at the halfway point, then dropped back to third going over formidable Becher's Brook. Jumping with great skill and courage, with young Hobbs guiding and rating him like a veteran, the little chestnut stallion was gaining on the leaders when he hit the third-to-last fence very hard and almost went down. Hobbs pulled him together and got going again, passing the second horse, Workman, as he stumbled going into the next fence. There remained only Royal Danieli to catch as he and Battleship approached the last fence; Royal Danieli cleared it two lengths in front, and his jockey, Dan Moore, elected to save ground and traverse the stretch close to the rail, forcing Battleship to take the middle of the track, which proved to offer firmer going. The two raced stride for stride to the finish, the little American's stride being somewhat longer (an inheritance from his long-striding sire, Man o' War) than that of his longer-legged opponent. A hundred yards from the finish, Battleship was still a half-length behind, but gaining, and the crowd was with him, urging him on. In the very last stride he caught Royal Danieli and won by a nose. The time, although not a record, was remarkably fast: 9 minutes 29 1/5 seconds, with the winner carrying 160 pounds.

No description of American participation in the Grand National can be considered complete without mention of two other entrants whose performances made sporting history. In the 1965 race, the winner, Jay Trump, was American-bred, American-owned and American-ridden. A nonwinner against the cheapest kind of competition on the flat track, he was sold by his breeder-owner-trainer to Mrs. Mary Stephenson of Cincinnati as a steeplechase prospect. Under amateur jockey Tommy Smith he progressed rapidly as a jumper, twice winning the Maryland Hunt Cup (the country's most prestigious race over fences) in record time and being selected as the steeplechase horse of the year. Jay Trump and Tommy Smith were then sent to England to get a year of racing experience in preparation for the Grand National, which they won by the narrowest of margins in one of the most exciting finishes ever seen at Aintree. Thus, thirty-seven years after Battleship's triumph, another American-bred horse won the coveted trophy, although many other Americans had tried for it in the intervening years.

Perhaps the best American-owned horse *never* to win the Grand National was Easter Hero, who had such ill fortune at Canal Turn in the 1928 race. In 1929 he was bought by John Hay Whitney, who was to become the United States Ambassador to the Court of St. James's many years later. A record field started the 1929 Grand National, with Easter Hero installed as the favorite. He was assigned a backbreaking impost of 175 pounds—a tremendous burden to carry in such a race. The starter got the field away quickly and safely, and Easter Hero went at once to the lead over the first fence—a lead which he maintained for the first four miles. Coming off Valentine's Brook the second time around, he was seen to be in trouble, galloping almost on three legs. With half a mile yet to go, Easter Hero was obviously in pain. Jockey Moloney was holding him together with a hand ride as the gallant favorite struggled on with shortening strides. Soon he was passed by Gregalach, a long-shot outsider, who went on to win. Easter Hero was pulled up immediately after crossing the finish line and the cause of his difficulty then became apparent. He had hit the top of a rail with his forefoot and his shoe had been twisted into an ''S'' shape, gashing his ankle at every stride and causing intense pain. A lesser horse would have quit, but Easter Hero was all heart and carried on with great courage in spite of the pain. For several years thereafter, Easter Hero's stall at Llangollen Farm in Virginia contained a plaque on which the twisted shoe was mounted. Visitors would marvel at the sight and shudder at the thought of the torturous pain the horse must have endured, and more than one sage horseman was heard to say, ''If I hadn't seen it, I wouldn't believe it.''

XVII
Hambletonian

Foundation Sire
of
Harness Racing

One sunny day in 1848 an Orange County, N.Y. farmer, Jonas Seely brought home to Sugar Loaf farm a crippled mare that had once belonged to his father and had fallen upon bad times. She had been too excitable to be trusted in harness for the elder Seely's purposes and, after one too many runaways, was sold to a New York butcher, Charley Kent, a drunkard and a heartless owner. Kent put the mare to work pulling a heavy wagon over the city cobblestones until she became permanently lamed and unable to work. He then sent her to auction and, by coincidence, she was sent back to Goshen to be slaughtered for meat. By chance, Jonas Seely found her in the local butcher's yard and, remembering the speed she had shown while running away with his sedate father, decided to mate her with one of the home stallions. Very probably he was also moved by sentiment to save the sorry-looking mare from being converted to dog meat. After all she had once been the pride of the Seely farm, and Jonas must have felt sad about the abuse she had endured after she had been sold.

Among the stallions standing at Sugar Loaf at that time was Abdallah, a Thoroughbred with a very undistinguished record as a racing trotter. Because he was reputed to have an ugly disposition and was known to be slow, he had not been patronized by the local owners of breeding mares. Seely, feeling that he had little to lose, bred the crippled mare to Abdallah. Eleven months later the union produced a gangling dark bay foal—destined to be the premier sire of trotters and pacers.

Apparently Seely was not impressed with Abdallah's colt, but his hired man, William Rysdyk, was a keen judge of horseflesh and felt the youngster had potential. He offered to buy the colt and, after some haggling, Jonas Seely offered Rysdyk a package deal—the colt and the crippled mare for $125. This was more money than Rysdyk had, so he made a counteroffer —to take the pair on a "pay later" basis—which Seely accepted. This transaction turned out to be the biggest bargain in the history of horsedom, for Hambletonian—as Rysdyk named the colt in honor

distrusted by many breeders. The prospects brightened considerably, however, in the following year, when Hambletonian was awarded not only the three-year-old championship at the Fair but also the grand stallion championship for all ages. Rysdyk promptly raised the fee to $10 with no guarantee, and the breeders responded with greatly increased interest and patronage.

By the time Hambletonian was a five-year-old, his progeny were being exhibited and winning at the Fair. To Rysdyk's delight, they were winning races against some of the best young trotters in the country, and he decided to retire from farming and concentrate solely on managing Hambletonian, whose fee was hiked to $25 per service. It was the first of a series of banner years for Rysdyk, for almost 100 mares came to Hambletonian's court that year and the ex-hired hand was on the way to becoming the Bank of Chester's wealthiest depositor.

All in all, Hambletonian spent twenty-four years in Rysdyk's stud, performing prodigies, and getting outstanding foals. As the colts and fillies he fathered gained fame at the races, Hambletonian's services became ever more in demand, and Rysdyk took advantage of the market; in 1864, when Hambletonian was fifteen, he was booked to 217 mares at a fee of $100; the following year the owners of 193 mares paid $300 each, and the unheard-of stud fee of $500 was gladly paid by 105 owners in 1865. The totals for this three-year period of activity, when Hambletonian was at the peak of his powers, are 515 mares and $132,100! The demand for Hambletonian's services was great and Rysdyk obviously worked the stallion to the limit of his capacity.

During his remarkable career as a stallion, spanning almost a quarter-century, Hambletonian produced over 1,300 foals out of the 1,900 mares sent to him. The failure of 600 mares to produce a foal should not be laid to the famous stallion, but rather to the quality of the barren mares. Rysdyk would accept any mare whose owner would pay the fee; hence many mares of dubious quality were accepted. What is significant about Hambletonian is the large number of foals he fathered that became outstanding performers on the track, both as pacers and as trotters; he stamped them with his own greatness and literally improved the breed.

Hambletonian died in 1876 at the advanced age of twenty-seven. In his later years his production slowed to the point where he could handle only thirty mares in a season, as compared with his peak year when almost 200 were serviced. At his demise he had long been recognized as the premier sire of trotters and pacers (a trotter picks his feet up and puts them down diagonally, as with the left front and right hind and then the other pair, whereas a pacer moves both legs on the same side at once). Because so many of his get were successful, and because they all resembled their sire in conformation, Hambletonian is credited with founding the Standardbred horse line (the breed name for trotters and pacers). Today 99 per cent of the Standardbreds registered throughout the world can trace their ancestry to this one outstanding progenitor. Some trotters now racing can trace as many as forty crosses to Hambletonian. To this very day (except for a brief period just before the turn of the century) every world's record holder for the mile trot or pace has been a Hambletonian descendant. Curiously, for the founder of a racing breed, Hambletonian himself never raced.

The Hambletonian Stake, which is to three-year-old Standardbred trotters what the Kentucky Derby is to their flat-racing Thoroughbred counterparts, is named for the founder of the breed and has become the one race most owners and trainers want to win. For many years it was held at Goshen, where Hambletonian was foaled; more recently the Du Quoin track in Illinois has been the site of this classic. The winner is the best performer in three heats of a mile each. Thus it is a more demanding test of a trotter than the races run nightly at the big name tracks such as Roosevelt and Yonkers raceways, where the public's interest in cashing bets and the state's avarice in collecting a high percentage of the total bet on each race have eliminated heat racing in favor of crowding as many races as possible into the program.

XVIII
Greyhound

World's Greatest Trotter

—

Greyhound was foaled in the spring of 1932 in Kentucky, a state not at that time noted as an important breeding area for the American Standardbred (the breed name for trotters and pacers). It was soon obvious that he was going to grow up taller than he was long. He was "close-coupled," an unpopular conformation with most horsemen of that era, who were convinced that a long body was the key to trotting speed. Grow tall he did, to 16½ hands or a full hand (four inches) more than the average for his breed. It was no wonder that he sold at auction as a yearling for a paltry $800, despite the fact that his sire was the noted Guy Abbey. Neither his breeder nor most of the bidders were much interested in a horse that did not exhibit the accepted dimensions popular at that time. Their mistake became evident when the grey gelding was sent to the track as a two-year-old and promptly began to out-trot everything in sight.

The history of harness racing, once merely a countryman's pastime, but now an important commercial sport, has many interesting aspects, one of the most unusual being that harness racing's development in America owes much to the religious beliefs of New Englanders. Reformers closed down the flat-racing tracks in New England around 1802, because they deemed racing to be immoral. The courts ruled, however, that trotting was not racing since a race is a contest to determine the fastest competitor and a trotter could go faster if he galloped! So "racing" was suspended for a time, during which trotting blossomed.

At first, trotting races, or "brushes," were not held at a track, but rather on straight roads laid out as speedways (Third Avenue in New York City was built as a speedway in 1807) and until 1830, trotting races were almost always held under saddle, rather than with a driver being pulled in a vehicle. Eventually tracks were built for trotters and a lightweight sulky was developed. The sport then became a horse-drawn contest much as we know it today, with the trotter harnessed to a two-wheeled sulky. As the sport became better organized, more attention began to be paid to breeding and there was much more careful selection of sires and dams with good racing records.

Morgans first dominated the field, but eventually all the best trotters were found to be descended from one stallion, Hambletonian, whose bloodlines traced to the Thoroughbred, Messenger. Hambletonian became the foundation sire of the modern trotter. One of his tenth generation descendants, Greyhound, became the greatest trotting horse the world has ever seen.

Colonel E. J. Baker of St. Charles, Illinois, and his astute trainer-driver, Sep Palin, soon realized that the Colonel had bought a potential champion; Greyhound took to training like a duck to water. His longer-than-average legs propelled him at a smooth, flowing, apparently effortless gait. His deep chest allowed plenty of room for oxygen, permitting him to go great distances before becoming winded. He was powerful and courageous and best of all, his stride of twenty-three feet was about three feet more than had ever been measured before. Furthermore, he was soft-mouthed and therefore adaptable to going at whatever speed Palin asked for, without wearing himself out by fighting the bit, as so many hard-mouthed pullers are apt to do. In harness, with the skillful Palin at the reins, he was capable of trotting thirty-five miles an hour in perfect stride. Greyhound was sent to the races as a two-year-old and won his first start. After placing and showing (track parlance for coming in second and third) in his next two starts, he won six straight, a record of seven wins in nine starts for the year. In one race, the Horseman's Futurity, he set a world's record for the fastest mile ever trotted by a two-year-old gelding—the first of twenty-five world's records he was to set in his seven-year racing career.

Greyhound's three-year-old campaign was a perfect performance. He raced only in major events, undefeated, and was unanimously selected three-year-old champion. Among his wins was the Hambletonian Stake, named for the foundation sire of the Standardbred breed of horses, and Greyhound's ancestor ten generations back. The Hambletonian is to harness racing what the Kentucky Derby is to flat racing, the premier event for three-year-olds and the contest that owners and trainers most want to win. The winner is the best in two out of three heats of a mile each; Greyhound won the first two heats with ease, and he and Sep Palin became overnight celebrities.

Campaigning as an older horse in the following years, the big grey was a consistent winner and crowd pleaser. Most trotters are bays and difficult to distinguish from each other due to their similar height and build. Greyhound was easily identifiable even to the most casual spectator because of his color, height and long stride. The fact that he was almost always in front of the pack from start to finish did not, of course, make it any harder for spectators to recognize him. The crowds came to see him win and he disappointed them only once (apart from his two non-winning races as a two-year-old when he was still green and needed experience). This defeat was on the half-mile track at Goshen, New York, the county seat of Orange County where Hambletonian founded the Standardbred line in the mid-1800's. The sharp turns and short straightaways of a half-mile track were not suited to Greyhound's big-going style and he lost a four-heat race by the closest of margins, winning the second heat, tying for first in the fourth and placing second in the other two. As if to compensate for letting his backers down, he trotted to a new world's record for a three-heat event a few days later on the Goshen mile track. In this, his four-year-old year, he won fifteen heats in seventeen starts, in one of which he set the world's record for the mile trotted by a four-year-old. In another start on a half-mile track he broke the world's record for that short distance, in spite of his aversion to the tight turns. By the time he retired in 1940, after seven years of competition, Greyhound had broken records for all distances from a quarter-mile up to and including two miles; he is officially credited with trotting the mile no less than twenty-five times in two minutes or less—an accomplishment that no other horse in history has even begun to approach. Probably 99 per cent of the thousands of trotters in training will never negotiate a two-minute mile.

Greyhound's times are still remarkable today, a third of a century later. Since his heyday, however, the heat has all but been abandoned, and it is no longer necessary for a driver to save his horse in the first heat in order to have enough left for the second or third. The development of synthetic racing surfaces has resulted in faster performances. Discoveries in veterinary science and a better knowledge of equine nutrition have helped to develop speed and staying power. The mobile starting gate, improved equipment, and less fatiguing means of transportation between tracks have all contributed to easier racing conditions and faster times. Greyhound had none of these latter-day benefits; a mile race for him today would be merely a sprint at full speed all the way, pulling a lighter sulky on a faster track under ideal racing conditions. Who can tell what fantastic records he might be setting if he were competing today?

To describe in detail all of Greyhound's accomplishments would require a separate book. However, certain highlights were so remarkable that no account of the great grey's career can ignore them. Preeminent, of course, was the mile record of 1:55¼ (one minute, fifty-five and a quarter seconds) which he set at Lexington, Kentucky, near his birthplace; the record stood for thirty-one years until it was barely broken by Nevele Pride in 1969. Greyhound's record was made in an exhibition, with no other horses on the track, whereas Nevele Pride had the advantage of two pacesetters, one for the first half and one to bring him home at predetermined speeds. In 1938, the same year in which he set the mile record, Greyhound also tied his own world's record of 1:57¼ for the mile in a scheduled race against other horses. And, to round out a banner year, he took ten seconds off the world's exhibition record for the mile and a half by trotting that distance in 3:02½.

After his triumphant four-year-old year, during which he became the acknowledged champion of champions, almost all of Greyhound's performances were exhibitions against time, for none of the other owners wanted to test their trotters against his overwhelming speed. Many times when Greyhound had been entered in a race, the other owners would "scratch" their horses and there would be no contest. In order to keep his champion racing, Colonel Baker was forced to seek somewhat out of the ordinary events for his horse. One such contest was staged at the 1939 New York State Fair at Syracuse, where Greyhound was put in double harness with Rosalind, the champion trotting mare that year. The pair pulled a sulky a mile in 1:59 to beat by 4¼ seconds the world's record that had been set in 1912. Not content to rest on these laurels, the pair repeated the feat five days later at Indianapolis in 1:58¼, a record that still stands.

At this point, there would seem to be no new worlds to conquer, but Colonel Baker found one—the mile trotted under saddle. This was to be Greyhound's last public appearance; owning all the records from a quarter-mile to two miles in harness, plus the record for pairs at a mile, the gallant grey would attempt to set the one record he had not heretofore attempted and, win or lose, it would be his finale. A leading horse-show rider of saddle horses, Mrs. Frances Dodge Johnson (later Mrs. Frederick Van Lennep, owner of Castleton Farm, which became a leading Standardbred producer), agreed to ride Greyhound over the Lexington track, although she had never ridden a trotter in a race or against time before. Thus both horse and rider were totally inexperienced in under-saddle, timed events.

The novelty of the attempt attracted widespread public attention both at home and abroad and, when Mrs. Johnson brought Greyhound to the finish in 2:01¾, three and a half seconds under the previous world's record, his immortality was assured. No other trotter—before or since—has even come close to Greyhound's versatile roster of triumphs.

Pacers (popularly known as "sidewheelers") are Standardbreds that move both legs on the same side at once, whereas the trot is a diagonal gait. Although many theories have been advanced, horsemen do not really understand why a pacer is faster than a trotter. Nevertheless, the record books reveal pacers' times to be faster than trotters' at almost any given distance. A good pacer will usually beat a good trotter in a match race. Late in September of 1939, a new world's pacing record was set by the great Standardbred, Billy Direct, who ran against the clock in a solo exhibition and completed the mile circuit in 1:55. A time trial of this nature can often produce better results than competition, because of a better start and the lack of interference from other horses. On the very next day after Billy Direct's record-breaking performance, Greyhound's owner—not content with holding the world's mile records in harness, both single and double, as well as under saddle—sent the grey gelding out to attempt the impossible. Greyhound was trotted an exhibition mile in an attempt to beat Billy Direct's pacing record, and came within a quarter of a second—a yard or two—of bringing it off. The time was no disgrace. It tied his previously set record of 1:55¼ made at Lexington two years earlier. It was the only goal Colonel Baker set for Greyhound that the champion trotter could not reach. Probably it should not have been attempted.

Although retired from competition in 1940, Greyhound was brought out from time to time to put on an exhibition in response to public interest; his last appearance was at the Grand Circuit meeting at Delaware, Ohio, as a fifteen-year-old in 1947. After that he held court for visitors at the Baker farm, enjoying the luxury of an unusually large stall, fifteen-by-thirty feet, in which he could be observed through a plate-glass window. In good health until shortly before his thirty-third birthday (very old for a horse) he died in February, 1965, and was buried in the farm's horse cemetery, where visitors still come to pay their respects. Even those who never saw him perform concede that Greyhound was the greatest trotter the world has ever seen.

XIX
Whirlaway

*Triple Crown
Winner*

In the heart of the Kentucky bluegrass region lies Calumet Farm, famous as a breeding farm and home of some of the finest stallions and brood mares in the world. Among the stallions standing at Calumet in 1937 was one considered truly great—Blenheim II; he had won the English Derby and then had been imported to America, where he sired many leading stakes winners. At Calumet he was mated to the good brood mare Dustwhirl, and the result of this union was Whirlaway, foaled in 1938—a chestnut colt with a diamond star on his forehead and an uncommonly long tail which was soon to become his trademark.

Kentucky bluegrass growing over limestone has long been recognized as the ideal grazing ground for young racehorses that are building bone and muscle to withstand the strains and stresses of competition when they are sent to the track as still-growing two-year-olds. A Thoroughbred does not reach full muscular maturity and bone strength until his fourth or fifth year; therefore, all the additional strength he can acquire through good grass and limestone water is of great importance to assure his being in the best possible condition when he leaves the breeding farm to begin a racing career.

Whirlaway's first year was spent grazing the lush bluegrass pastures, running and playing with the other Calumet foals born that year and generally enjoying a carefree life. The farmhands, ever alert to spot a promising prospect, soon noticed that the young colt (he had not yet been named, and was referred to as Dustwhirl's colt) had more speed and was more aggressive than his fellow youngsters. This information was conveyed to the farm's new trainer, Ben Jones.

In the years to follow, the names of Whirlaway and Ben Jones were to become inseparable; did Ben Jones the superb trainer make Whirlaway famous or did the big chestnut bring fame to Ben Jones? This debate, which frequently arose wherever horsemen gathered, was usually resolved by agreement that each contributed to the other's reputation in equal measure. Certainly no ordinary trainer could have extracted as much performance from Whirlaway as Jones did, for the son of Blenheim II inherited much of his sire's bad disposition and at times as many as four grooms were required to get a saddle on his back.

Whirlaway proved difficult to train, not liking to go between horses and the rail. He performed best when allowed to trail the pack and then turn on a burst of blinding speed in the home stretch, catching and passing horses as he raced down the middle of the track. This, of course, is a difficult and risky way to win a race; Whirlaway in the middle of the track had more distance to cover than had the horses on the rail. His dislike of taking the lead caused problems for his jockey. It took a highly experienced and smart rider to know just when to take the big chestnut to the outside and turn him loose; if too late, the leaders could not be caught in time, and if too soon, he might become too winded and falter at the finish from the effort of his great burst of speed.

Whirlaway showed his great potential by winning his first start at Lincoln Fields near Chicago on June 3, 1940. Convinced that he had a good colt, Jones took him to Arlington Park—a major track offering first-class competition—where the long-tailed youngster won one race out of five entered. In each case he started his run from behind the field and refused to take the short route on the rail. Although he lost four races, it was generally observed that Whirlaway was the fastest horse in the race and could have won under a more astute jockey, one with a highly developed sense of timing and a better knowledge of his colt's capabilities.

Notwithstanding this rather inauspicious beginning, Ben Jones had faith in his fast two-year-old, realizing that both he and the colt could learn how to beat slower horses; for at full tilt Whirlaway was unquestionably the fastest of all two-year-olds in training. The problem was how to let him run as he pleased in the early stages of a race, and then start the drive for home at the right time, avoiding the rail.

The lessons from the losing races at Arlington had been well learned by the time the Calumet string arrived at Saratoga in upstate new York, where the best two-year-old racing in the country is held each August. In his first start there, in the United States Hotel Stakes, a major two-year-old event, Whirlaway finished second, going fastest at the finish but not quite catching the winner in time. In his next race, the Saratoga Special—a sweepstakes with the winner taking all of the purse—he came from fourteen lengths behind to win and attract the attention of the crowd. By this time his tail had become so long as to nearly reach his ankles and the sight of the big chestnut coming from behind with his long tail streaming made him an easy horse for spectators to identify.

After losing his next start by beginning his stretch drive too late, Whirlaway came back to win the Saratoga Cup in the mud, showing his versatility under difficult racing conditions.

Whirlaway ended his first year on the track as the leading two-year-old money-winner in the country, having entered sixteen races, won seven and been out of the money only four times. Obviously he was a leading candidate for three-year-old honors; rather than wear him out at the winter tracks, Jones sent him back to Calumet Farm to rest and grow in anticipation of a long campaign the following year.

In 1941 Ben Jones set dead aim on Whirlaway's winning the Triple Crown of racing for

three-year-olds—the Kentucky Derby, Preakness and Belmont—a feat previously accomplished by only four horses—Sir Barton, Gallant Fox, Omaha and War Admiral, all great racers. The Derby comes early in the spring before horses normally are at their peak. The Preakness is run shortly thereafter, followed by the long mile-and-a-half Belmont Stakes. Many good horses had assayed the challenge, and all but four had fallen short, either from bad racing luck or injury. Whirlaway was entered in seven races preceding the Derby, but was not asked to extend himself in them. Ben Jones was more interested in conditioning his horse for the big events than in winning lesser races at the expense of straining his hopeful. Although not under stress, Whirlaway won three of these "training trial" races and came close in the others. When Derby Day at Churchill Downs in Kentucky came in May, he was fit and ready to run a mile and a quarter for the first time. The race was hardly a contest for the little chestnut with the flowing tail; he came from well back to win by eight lengths going away, setting a new track (and Derby) record of 2:01 2/5, and delighting the crowd that made him an overwhelming favorite. He then was shipped to Baltimore, where he won the Preakness by five and a half lengths. Having won the first two legs of the Triple Crown, Whirlaway automatically became the center of public attention, and interest was high in the colt's attempt to secure the third leg. Whirlaway made an easy conquest of the Belmont in June, thereby joining a very select company of horses. From that time on a mention of "Mr. Longtail" would bring instant recognition even among those who do not normally follow racetrack news.

In the middle of his four-year-old year, campaigning as an older horse and giving away weight to all his competitors, Whirlaway won the Massachusetts Handicap and became the all-time money-winner, displacing the famous Seabiscuit. The total, $454,376, seems unimpressive today, but it should be remembered that purses in those halcyon days were relatively small, and the era of the $100,000 race was still in the future; had Whirlaway won the same events a quarter of a century later, his winnings would have been over the $5-million mark.

During his years on the track, Whirlaway raced against several good horses, including Market Wise, Fenelon, Swing and Sway, Bolingbroke, Challedon, Devil Diver and Alsab. Of this outstanding crop of stakes winners his principal rival for celebrity status was the rags-to-riches Alsab, whose life story fascinated the public and made good copy for the sportswriters. Alsab was an unfashionably bred yearling bought at auction for $700 by a Chicago politician, Albert Sabath, who was sufficiently lacking in modesty to name the colt for himself (considered bad luck by horsemen).

Chicago politicians in those days were apt to have unsavory reputations, and the general feeling at the track was that Sabath would hardly qualify as a pillar of the turf—a judgment that Alsab's owner did nothing to controvert. He retained "Sarge" Schwenk, a trainer of cheap horses who was noted for working them hard and often, and Schwenk soon had Alsab running for his oats. The only thing that turned out to be "cheap" about Alsab was his price at auction, for Sabath and Schwenk soon found out that their new acquisition was not only dead game, but had great speed and stamina. As a tender two-year-old he was raced twenty-two times and given no rest before embarking on an even more strenuous three-year-old career. His management was indifferent to the frequently publicized charge that they were "killing the goose that laid the golden egg," and raced him almost weekly against top company. The wonder of the sporting world was how any horse could stand up under such grueling treatment, but Alsab was genuinely an iron horse and kept going. On the few occasions when the strain became too much, Schwenk would patch him up and send him back to the races in short order to run again, a practice which appalled those who felt that a flesh and blood horse is something more than a money-making machine.

Alsab's record, while not as glamorous as Whirlaway's, was impressive. He had won the Preakness and several other stakes, in one of which he ran the fastest recorded mile of the year. Like Whirlaway, he loved to come from behind to challenge in the homestretch. The two had never raced each other, and great public interest developed in a match race at Narragansett Park in Rhode Island at one and a sixteenth miles. The conditions were weight for age, with Whirlaway toting 126 pounds and Alsab 119, for a winner-take-all purse of $25,000. The public's interest was understandable, to say the least; this was to be a classic confrontation of two great and highly publicized horses—overworked, badly managed and mishandled Alsab from the wrong side of the tracks versus fashionably owned and superbly handled Whirlaway, the Triple Crown winner and leading money-winner.

Unlike so many contests where anticipation exceeds realization, the Alsab-Whirlaway match race was a thriller from start to finish. Jockey Carroll Bierman took Alsab to the front at the start, with Whirlaway tagging along a length behind. After three quarters of a mile George Woolf made his bid with Whirlaway, but Alsab hung on to his slight lead as both horses ran all out down the homestretch. Whirlaway gradually closed the gap, gaining inches at each stride, as the finish was approached, and it appeared that the race was a dead heat. After long deliberation and study of the photo finish, the judges awarded the race to Alsab, but both horses were credited with identical times. The consensus of most horsemen who witnessed the race was that Bierman's strategy had paid off; by setting a fast pace at the start he forced Woolf on Whirlaway to stay with him and drained some of the reserve strength that normally the longtailed champion could call on to sustain a whirlwind finish. Jockey Woolf was afraid to drop too far back for fear that Alsab would "steal" the race with his front-running tactics, and Whirlaway was therefore not allowed to run the come-from-behind race which was his preference.

The two met again later in the year in the two-mile Jockey Club Gold Cup, in which Whirlaway was allowed to run the way he liked best. Restrained for the first mile and a half, he turned on the speed in the backstretch and caught front-running Alsab a furlong (one eighth of a mile) from the finish, gradually drawing ahead to win by three quarters of a length. Whirlaway raced well as a four-year-old, bringing his winnings up over the half million dollar mark, but some of the old closing speed was gone as the result of an injury. When he failed to respond to a careful training program as a five-year-old, he was retired to stud and returned to his birthplace, Calumet

Farm, to begin a career as a sire. His retirement was marked by a proclamation by the Governor of Kentucky naming August 8, 1943, as "Whirlaway Day," a well-deserved tribute to the long-tailed little horse who was unquestionably the best known and most popular racehorse since the one and only Man o' War.

Before Whirlaway had much opportunity to prove his worth as a sire, a leading French breeder, Marcel Boussac, leased him in an effort to rebuild the Thoroughbred stock that had been so sadly downgraded during the war. Whirlaway's first crop of foals in France were a promising lot, but his career overseas was abruptly terminated when he died suddenly in 1953 of a rupture.

Whirlaway's racing career extended over the better part of four seasons; he started sixty times, almost always in top company; won thirty-two, and was out of the money only four times (and those in his first year of racing). He was the leading money-winner during each of his first three racing years, and was Horse of the Year twice. He carried high weight—often giving more than thirty pounds to his competitors—and won stakes at distances from seven furlongs to two miles. He was one of the élite handful of Triple Crown winners. This record alone is more than sufficient for Hall of Fame recognition, but Whirlaway had something else that made him stand out from the crowd and be remembered today when other horses of similiar caliber have been forgotten—it was his sensational come-from-behind rush in the homestretch, with his long tail flowing, that thrilled the audience and endeared him to the sporting public. He never ran a bad race, and almost all of them were undecided until the final strides, with the racegoers in suspense as they wondered whether he could get to the front in time. As a crowd-pleaser and thrill-provider he had no equal.

XX
Canonero II
Surprise
Kentucky Derby
Winner

Churchill Downs racetrack in Louisville, home of the famous Kentucky Derby, has seen many strange sights in its long history, but probably nothing before or since will ever compare with the tumultuous throng of South Americans—most of them speaking little or no English—who crowded into the winner's circle in 1971 in adulation of a brown colt that few people had ever heard of five minutes before. The horse to win their voluble affection had never raced in the United States until he won $145,000 as the unexpected victor in the most surprising of all the ninety-seven Derbies.

The story of Canonero II, the brown three-year-old winner's name, begins near Paris, Kentucky, in the bluegrass region, where a very unfashionable mare named Dixieland II gave birth to an unimpressive colt sired by a little-known stallion, Pretendre—a horse that had never amounted to much in his racing days and had absolutely no reputation in the stud. The colt's breeder, Edward Benjamin, was probably delighted to see Canonero go for $1,200 (a small amount for a well-bred yearling) at the Keeneland sales auction of yearlings in 1969. There were few bidders for the little brown colt and his new owner, Edgar Caibett, considered him too inferior a prospect for racing in the United States. Instead he was taken to race in Caibett's native Venezuela, where racing is not on as high a competitive level as it is in the United States.

Although Caibett was the owner of record (perhaps because he spoke a few words of English), Canonero's actual owner was Pedro Baptista, Caibett's father-in-law, a well-to-do plumbing contractor in Caracas. Baptista apparently had little interest in racing, and the Canonero racing career in South America was largely in the hands of jockey Gustavo Avila and Caibett. Trainer Juan Arias was relatively unknown even in his native country.

Americans tend to scoff at the methods used to train horses by long, slow workouts such as Canonero underwent in Venezuela. But many American horses are burned out by too much early racing and finished before they are fully grown, victims of being brought along too fast and asked to do too much too soon. Horses brought along more slowly and not overextended at too early an age are more apt to develop soundly and strongly and to have longer careers as older horses.

By American standards, Canonero's training would seem to be archaic. His exercise boy would ride him for many hours each day at slow work, either bareback or with a small blanket in place of a saddle. Consequently Canonero's disposition was never taxed and he was handy at any gait, responsive to his rider's commands. The slow workouts developed muscle and wind, gradually building the colt's endurance to the point where he could gallop five or more miles at speed with no discomfort, something few horses in our country can do.

Late in his second year, Canonero was sent to the Caracas races, where his performance was more than satisfactory, if not especially notable. In that salubrious climate where snow and cold are unknown, he was kept fit all during the winter and was in fine shape as spring approached. About this time, his owner of record, Caibett, decided that a junket to the United States was in order, and the family agreed that it would be great fun to bring Canonero along and enter him in the Kentucky Derby, the race most horse owners (as distinguished from horsemen) would like to win for the accompanying social prestige and publicity. The Derby is such a magnet for social-climbing owners, that many horses with no chance of winning are entered to satisfy their owners' vanity. However, the Caibetts, the trainer and the jockey all felt that Canonero had at least a fair chance to comport himself without disgrace, since his won/lost record in racing was the best of all those entered in the race; he had six wins to his credit and obviously was not a run-of-the-mill campaigner in his own country.

Canonero's entry was received at Churchill Downs with no great enthusiasm. As an American-bred horse exported as inferior to his fellow Kentuckians, he was regarded with little or no interest. The track handicapper quoted his chances at 300 to 1, extremely and unusually long odds. This indifference was shared by the sports reporters, who ignored his record in Venezuela on the assumption that racing near the equator was quite inferior to that on our own tracks. Compounding the indifference was the fact that Canonero left Venezuela by air only nine days before the race and had to spend four days in a quarantine stall at Miami before going on to Louisville; thus he was in the country only a little more than four days before the race, hardly time to get acclimated.

In the pre-race publicity, Canonero received virtually no mention other than a few jesting paragraphs featuring the fact that neither his trainer nor his jockey spoke English. The language barrier got more lines than the horse, purely as a piece of curiosity and interest. About the only consideration extended to the Canonero entourage was made by George Poole, who was training two horses for the Derby. Taking pity on his fellow trainer, Juan Arias, Poole lent him a Puerto Rican groom, Santiago García as an interpreter. García was astounded at the casual preparations for the big race and, to his everlasting regret, declined to wager on the South American entry, saying that the big brown was too fat.

On the day of the race, twenty horses were to start. Since the tote board did not have twenty

spaces, six horses—including Canonero—were lumped in the "field," a polite euphemism for the most lightly regarded starters. The favorite, Unconscious, went off at 3 to 1, whereas any horse in the field would pay 6 to 1 to win, and Canonero, if there had been no field group, would very probably have gone off at 100 to 1 or higher. As the race progressed, Canonero rallied from eighteenth position to beat Jim French, the second favorite, by almost four lengths. Then came pandemonium as well-wishers, reporters and television announcers all crowded around the Venezuelans. The interviewers spoke no Spanish, the Venezuelans no English and García was nowhere to be found; neither trainer Arias nor jockey Avila could communicate with the interviewers, and Edgar Caibett was too overwhelmed to muster any of his limited English.

The bizarre circumstances surrounding Canonero's winning of the Derby created headlines far beyond the usual publicity given to that notable race, and interest ran high when it was announced that he would be entered in the Preakness at Pimlico racetrack in Baltimore. The Preakness is the second jewel in the mythical Triple Crown series which has been won only by a mere handful of the many good horses that have attempted to attain it.

Sportscasters and reporters filled many columns of copy on Canonero—was his win of the Derby a freak, a once-in-a-lifetime Cinderella-like performance? Could he come from behind as he did in the Derby to win on Pimlico's shorter homestretch? What of his curious and seemingly lackadaisical training schedule? Why had his real owner, Señor Baptista, not bothered to come to the Derby and watch his horse triumph? Was Canonero really a first-class racehorse or had he just been lucky in beating a mediocre lot of three-year-olds? Many were the skeptics unwilling to believe the evidence that the unknown horse actually was a good one. The Preakness would tell if the South American was a freak and the whole country waited for the Preakness with a greater intensity of interest than ever before known for a horserace.

Canonero was trained as casually as ever for this second start on American soil, with jockey Avila giving slow, random gallops—riding bareback or on a pad but never in a saddle or using stirrups. The hard-boot American trainers, accustomed to working their horses at speed, could not believe that the South Americans were taking their task seriously. But unperturbed, and unable to communicate except with each other, the Canonero contingent maintained the relaxed style that had characterized their conduct two weeks earlier in Kentucky, before instant fame struck them.

Canonero drew post position nine for the Preakness, an outside position among the ten starters in the race. Most jockeys would drop back to the rail and follow the pack around the first turn, thinking that a lesser evil than asking their mount for a quick early effort to break fast and cut across in front of the inside starters in order to get on the rail. It was therefore expected that Canonero's post position would dictate a repeat of his Derby race—following the leaders until within striking distance of the finish and then turning on a burst of speed in an attempt to come from behind. To every Yankee's surprise, Canonero broke first out of the gate and led all the way to the wire, setting a new record time for the race, 2/5 of a second under the great Nashua's time of 1:54 2/5. He was clocked for the mile in 1:35, or 2 2/5 seconds faster than the Pimlico record for that distance. In his first two starts he had won a total of $282,400 for four minutes work and in his second race had established himself in the doubters' minds as a truly fine racer. Never before had an unknown horse scored such spectacular triumphs and made the jump from obscurity to worldwide fame as a two-race winner.

By now Canonero was a popular favorite to win the Belmont, the final race in the Triple Crown for three-year-olds. No longer were the casual training methods scoffed at by rival horse-men. It seemed as if the entire continents of North and South America were rooting for him and there appeared to be no horse in sight to give him a good challenge in his third start; in fact many of his opponents in the Derby and Preakness declined to oppose him in the Belmont. If ever there was a shoo-in for the Belmont, it had to be Canonero; many a racegoer must have felt that a bet on the brown favorite offered greater reward and no less security than the purchase of a government bond.

Canonero started the Belmont as an odds-on favorite, quoted at 3 to 5, while 81,000 spectators—a record track attendance—watched. He led at the end of the first mile, as expected; then tired and finished fourth behind Pass Catcher, a 35-to-1 outsider. Again pandemonium reigned but for a different reason. What had happened? That question was on everyone's lips. Rumors flew in all directions, the most popular being either that the horse had been drugged or the jockey's life threatened. The explanation, as dragged out by an interpreter from the reluctant trainer, Arias, was somewhat less dramatic. The quarantine stall at Miami was unclean, and Canonero had contracted a fungus infection while confined there. The fungus spread as time went by and infected Canonero's off (right) hind leg so that he had to be taken out of training for treatment a few days before the Belmont. Not wanting to disappoint the horse's newly found fans, Arias did not disclose the circumstances, although he realized that Canonero could not possibly live up to his two previous brilliant performances. The trainer's secrecy was, of course, a serious error of judgement. He gambled on Canonero being able to last the route against inferior horses and lost—a disservice both to the horse and to his backers.

Canonero never raced again. Shortly after the Belmont fiasco he was retired and purchased for the stud at a reputed figure of one million dollars, quite an improvement over his purchase price of a mere $1,200 before his brief but spectacular rise to fame.

XXI
Secretariat
Record-setting
Triple Crown
Winner

Old-timers all agree that Secretariat, the 1973 Triple Crown winner, was the "best-made" race horse ever to run on a track. Certainly his conformation was nearly perfect; the big handsome son of Bold Ruler and Somethingroyal was a true picture horse with his bright red chestnut coat, intelligent eye, classic sculptured head, big-barreled muscular body and long clean legs. His noted trainer, Lucien Laurin, once remarked, "He was so good looking when I got him that I said to myself he probably won't be worth ten cents as a racer." Happily for Mr. Laurin, the good-looking colt more than lived up to his promise and became the greatest racehorse since the days when Citation won the Triple Crown—a feat unduplicated until Secretariat pulled it off twenty-five years later.

What were the conformation features that caught trainer Laurin's eye, as well as those of the knowledgeable horsemen who watched Secretariat in the paddock and on the track? Let's look at the handsome stallion in profile and discuss his features, with emphasis on the factors contributing to stamina and speed, in the same sequence of examination that Laurin might be expected to use: First of all, a horse should be pleasing to the eye, with no grotesque features, harmoniously put together with the various sections of his body in correct proportion to each other. A well-built horse "fills the eye," and Secretariat certainly meets this requirement. The next question to be answered by offhand observation is whether he is built to run fast; the rule of thumb here is to compare the body length (from chest to rump) with the height (measured from the withers, or prominent bone at the base of the neck, to the ground). Height should exceed length, as Secretariat's does. A horse so constructed is said to "stand over a lot of daylight;" a horse with body longer than height carries a disproportionate amount of weight on his hindquarters thus overloading the legs that are the propelling force.

Now to a more detailed inspection; first, and most important, are the legs, for nothing else matters if they cannot do the job. Secretariat's legs are clean, without blemish, and well under him so that he is in balance. The pasterns (the short sections just above the hoof) slope at just about the right angle (35°) to act as shock absorbers and to provide a spring that lengthens the stride. Shorter and stumpier pasterns would shorten the stride and not absorb shocks as well, longer or more sloping pasterns would be mechanically weak and tend to cause a breakdown under strain. Long cannon bones (the sections of the legs from the knee or hock to the fetlock joint at the top of the pastern) are a great asset for speed, particularly if they are naturally vertical; Secretariat's cannons are remarkably long and his hind legs are exceptionally superior in all respects. Remembering that the hind legs provide the power and propulsion, it is evident that Secretariat's legs are constructed to provide great speed.

The shoulder is one of the most important features of a racehorse, since a long sloping shoulder enables a long stride at the gallop (trotters have straighter shoulders, and cart horses have shoulders that are almost vertical). Secretariat's shoulder, which extends from the withers to the chest at the base of the neck, provides a large area for leg muscle attachment at the proper angle for fast work at an extended stride.

So far we have observed the points of conformation contributing to a racehorse's speed—a favorable height in proportion to body length, well-set pasterns, long straight lower legs, and a long sloping shoulder—all of which Secretariat has in great and pleasing measure. But the ability to run a distance—the difference between a sprinter and a stayer—depends on whether the heart can pump enough oxygen through the bloodstream to the muscles to sustain prolonged effort. Secretariat's deep chest and well-sprung ribs give ample room for the lungs to contract and expand in order to provide the heart with sufficient oxygen, and his well-defined windpipe is large enough to carry the air breathed in by his large nostrils. Very definitely his body conformation indicates the ability to sustain physical effort over a long distance. The broad forehead is not only an indicator of intelligence (it provides brain space) but is also another guarantee of ability to take in sufficient air, because the frontal portion forms the roof under which the air passes en route to the lungs.

Inasmuch as the perfectly made horse has yet to be foaled, a comment on Secretariat's one conformation fault, a very minor one, is in order. He is slightly "goose rumped", i.e., his hindquarters slope a little too much because his pelvis is a bit out of line. This can be an aid in jumping, and it is probable that Secretariat could have been a great steeplechaser if he had ever been put to jumping fences. But a goose rump is not an attribute for speed, although obviously in Secretariat's case it was no deterrent to winning races.

Secretariat was owned by The Meadow Farm in Doswell, Virginia, the estate of Christopher Chenery, a utilities magnate. The Chenery family had owned The Meadow before the Civil War, but it had passed into other hands during the aftermath of that tragic conflict which brought financial reverses to so many of the South's proud families. A self-made man, Mr. Chenery fulfilled a lifetime ambition when business success enabled him to buy The Meadow and satisfy his longtime desire to engage in breeding and racing. Shortly after Secretariat was foaled, Mr.

Chenery died—not long after his retirement from The Meadow—and the duties of running the farm were assumed by his gracious and attractive daughter, Mrs. Helen ("Penny") Tweedy. By virtue of her association with Secretariat, Penny Tweedy was shortly to become almost as much of a television celebrity as her famous horse; her poise in leading him to the winner's circle, her gleeful modesty in accepting his trophies, and her unassuming candidness in giving all credit to trainer Laurin and jockey Ron Turcotte endeared her to millions of viewers who were captivated by her charm and business acumen.

Had it not been for a lucky flip of a coin, Secretariat would have been the property of Ogden Phipps, master of the renowned Wheatley Stable, chairman of the Jockey Club and owner of Bold Ruler, the greatest American sire of modern times. Messrs. Phipps and Chenery had a long-standing agreement that two Chenery mares could be bred to Bold Ruler each year, with Mr. Phipps retaining one of the resulting foals as payment for both stud fees. The choice of foals, by custom, was decided by a coin toss. Mrs. Tweedy, as her father's agent, called "tails" and took Somethingroyal's foal back to The Meadow. This must have been the world's most lucrative flip of a 50-cent piece, for within three years the foal, now named Secretariat, had won more than a million dollars on the track and was syndicated at stud for more than six million! Ironically for Mr. Phipps, the other foal, a filly named The Bride, was a total nonentity—one of the few of Bold Ruler's get that couldn't even earn enough to pay the feed bill.

Secretariat went to the races as a promising two-year-old and turned in some sensational performances after losing his first race when he got into a traffic jam at the start and had to run around horses; although obviously the best, he could not get to the front in the short sprint distance. He finished first in all his other starts, but was disqualified in the Champagne Stakes (a prestigious event for youngsters held each year at Saratoga) for crossing over and interfering with the horse that was then declared the winner. In the record book for 1972 Secretariat is credited with winning seven of his nine races and earning $456,404 to gain the two-year-old championship. He was also named Horse of the Year, a distinction never before conferred on a two-year-old.

Although The Meadow stable was operating profitably under Mrs. Tweedy's management, the death of her father was followed by serious problems in settling his estate and paying off the taxes which the government levied against Mr. Chenery's substantial business earnings. In order to resolve the matter, the decision was made to sell Secretariat and his older stablemate, the very good racer Riva Ridge. Secretariat's superior breeding, great conformation and impressive racing record obviously made him valuable as a sire, provided he was potent, but he had only raced one year and Mrs. Tweedy wanted him to run as a three-year-old—particularly in pursuit of the coveted Triple Crown of racing—the Kentucky Derby, Preakness, and Belmont Stakes. She also wanted Riva Ridge to take a shot at the major races for four-year-olds and up. It was a gamble, of course, for an unforeseen injury could cancel out, or reduce, the value of the horses. On the other hand, another successful racing season would materially increase the stud fee. A deal was worked out, with the aid of Seth Hancock, of Claiborne Farm in Paris, Kentucky, for the horses to be syndicated at the end of the 1973 season. An astonishing world's record amount was paid by bidders for a share of Secretariat, a total of thirty-two shares were sold at $190,000 each; Mrs. Tweedy obtained four shares and was guaranteed $5,320,000 from the remaining twenty-eight shares, subject, of course, to Secretariat's surviving the racing season and proving fertile. For his $190,000, each shareholder was entitled to send one mare a year to Secretariat; one of the first purchasers was Ogden Phipps, who had lost the coin toss that sent Secretariat to The Meadow stable rather than to his own Wheatley establishment The shareholders were not entitled to any of Secretariat's winnings from racing, so Mrs. Tweedy still had an entire racing season ahead of her with full ownership of the world's most valuable horse.

Secretariat's three-year-old racing career was a brilliant one. The public, fascinated by his syndication for such a large price and overwhelmed by the intense media coverage to which he was subjected, considered him to be a super horse, which he very nearly was. People who had never been to the races, many of whom would not have been able to tell the difference between a paddock and a pastern, became instant experts in debating whether Secretariat was a better horse than Citation or even Man o' War (a little like arguing whether Muhammed Ali could have beaten Joe Louis or Jack Dempsey). Even the usually austere *New York Times* got into the act with an article comparing the price of an ounce of gold (which was going through a rapid inflationary rise and was about to hit $100) with the value of a pound of Secretariat ($5,417, obtained by dividing his weight into the syndication price plus his 1972 earnings).

Fans of Secretariat had hoped that the great horse would retire undefeated. In the rare instances when he was beaten in 1973 he always had valid excuses. In the Wood Memorial, considered to be a good test of Kentucky Derby hopefuls, he was given a bad ride by jockey Turcotte, who freely admitted that he should have let the big chestnut run faster at the start of the race. And he was beaten by a horse named Onion, to whom he conceded a lot of weight, in a minor race on a day when he was "off his feed" and Onion was very fit. Trainer Laurin later admitted that Secretariat was not in top shape, but needed a race and was entered because Laurin underestimated the competition. The next time they met, Secretariat put Onion away with great authority. And Ron Turcotte, a truly fine jockey, never again made the mistake of not letting Secretariat run whenever he indicated impatience with a slow pace.

As time for the Kentucky Derby approached, there were a few doubters who, remembering the loss in the Wood, questioned whether Secretariat could win at a mile and a quarter, a distance he had never raced before. But the general public made him the betting favorite and a record crowd of 130,000 came to see him win, which he did very decisively by setting a new record of 1:59 2/5 to win the first leg of the Triple Crown. Next was the Preakness, which he won by going around tired horses in a great surge of speed that again set a record, according to all timers except the official clock, of 1:53 2/5 for the mile and three sixteenths. It was later determined that the official track clock was faulty, but the Maryland Racing Commissioners regretfully announced that they could not accept unofficial timing and the inaccurate result would have to stand. Mrs. Tweedy, always the complete lady under all circumstances, merely smiled and told the commission, "I understand, and sympathize with you. You're stuck with it."

By the deadline for paying the final starting fee for the Belmont, the third and final race for the Triple Crown, Secretariat had scared off all but a handful of his challengers, and a small field of five went to the post. There were no doubters when the mile and a half race ended two minutes and twenty-four seconds later, for Secretariat had broken the event's record while winning by the incredible margin of thirty-one lengths. At the mile and a quarter, with the toughest quarter mile yet to go, he beat his own Kentucky Derby record time by 2/5 of a second. At the finish, his winning time was 2 3/5 seconds better than the old track record set by Gallant Man. Not only was this a new record for the Belmont, it set a new track record and a new American record. If Secretariat had been given any competition in the last quarter mile, instead of being eased up, his time would unquestionably have been even more remarkable. Secretariat was only the ninth horse to win the Triple Crown since Sir Barton first won it in 1919, fifty-four years earlier. The last previous winner, to whom Secretariat is most frequently compared, was Citation in 1948, a quarter of a century earlier. Truly, Secretariat earned a place in the top flight of American racing greats, and his place in the Racing Hall of Fame is assured for all time.

By now public interest in Secretariat was so intense that a cigarette manufacturer offered to put up a $250,000 purse for a match race between Secretariat and his stablemate, Riva Ridge, who had won the Kentucky Derby and Belmont the year before but had bad luck in the Preakness. The two had never raced each other; Riva Ridge was having a very good year, and there was speculation as to whether the younger horse could beat Mrs. Tweedy's other superb racehorse. There was some criticism of a race between two horses under the same ownership, so the event—the Marlboro Cup—was made an invitational affair and seven of the country's best horses started in the one and one-eighth mile handicap. Secretariat answered the question by beating Riva Ridge (who finished second) by three and a half lengths while setting a world's record of 1:45 2/5 for the distance.

In his final race, the Canadian International Championship at Woodbine Park, Ontario, Secretariat closed out his career in style, winning that searching test of a mile and five-eighths for the richest purse ever offered in Canada. It was a sloppy, slippery run on turf on a mean, rainy and gusty day, which did not deter a record crowd from coming out to cheer the favorite. Ron Turcotte, who had ridden Secretariat in all but two of his twenty-one races, had been "set down" by the New York stewards for rough riding a few days before, so Secretariat's final ride was under the capable hands of Eddie Maple, who normally was up on Riva Ridge, the other great Tweedy campaigner. So ended on a high note one of the most remarkable racing careers of all time; because he ran only a relatively few races, Secretariat did not come near the earnings record mark but his two-year lifetime total of $1,306,818 is still an impressive one—averaging a bit more than $62,200 per race.

Having closed out one chapter in his career, Secretariat had now to begin a second career as a sire. Since the syndicate sale hinged on whether he was fertile, he was sent to Seth Hancock's farm for testing, as was Riva Ridge. To the consternation of Mrs. Tweedy and the twenty-eight other shareholders, first test results were negative, and it appeared that The Meadow might have to refund $190,000 to each shareholder—a financial disaster for the Chenery estate. Eventually, after Secretariat settled down and completely unwound from his racing tensions, he managed to get a trial mare—an Appaloosa named Leola—in foal. Early in November, 1974, the product of this mating was born in Winona, Minnesota, a red chestnut colt with Appaloosa spots on his hindquarters and with a white blaze on his face and three white socks just like his daddy's. Meanwhile, on the strength of this first success, Secretariat was bred to the mares of most of the shareholders. Mrs. Tweedy's big gamble had paid off handsomely.

Selected Bibliography

Alexander, David, *A Sound of Horses*. Indianapolis: Bobbs Merrill, 1966.

Blackford, William W., *War Years With Jeb Stuart*. New York: Scribner's, 1945

Busby, Hamilton, *The Trotting and the Pacing Horse in America*. New York: MacMillan, 1904.

Crowell, Pers, *Cavalcade of American Horses*. New York: 1951.

Davis, Deering, *The American Cow Pony*. Princeton: Van Nostrand, 1962.

Dobie, Frank J., *The Mustangs*. Boston: Little, Brown, 1952.

Downey, Fairfax, *Horses of Destiny*. New York: Scribner's, 1949.

Dustin, Fred, *The Custer Myth*. Harrisburg: Stackpole, 1953.

Fee, Chester A., *Chief Joseph*. New York: Wilson-Erickson, 1939.

Forbes, Esther, *Paul Revere and the World He Lived In*. Boston: Houghton Mifflin, 1942.

Freeman, Douglas S., *George Washington* (4 vols). New York: Scribner's, 1948-51.

—*Lee's Lieutenants* (3 vols). New York: Scribner's, 1942-44.

—*R. E. Lee* (4 vols). New York: Scribner's 1934-35.

Gettemy, Charles F., *The True Story of Paul Revere*. Boston: Little, Brown, 1906.

Goodall, Daphne M., *Horses of the World*. New York: MacMillan, 1965.

Graham, W. A., *The Story of the Little Big Horn*. New York: 1926.

Haines, Francis, *Appaloosa*. Austin, Texas: University of Texas Press, 1963.

— *Horses in America*. New York: Crowell, 1971.

Hergesheimer, Joseph, *Sheridan*. Boston: Houghton Mifflin, 1931.

Herr, John K. and Wallace, Edward S., *The Story of the U.S. Cavalry*. Boston: Little, Brown, 1953.

Howard, Robert, *Hoofbeats of Destiny*. New York: Signet, 1960.

—*The Horse in America*. Chicago: Follett, 1965.

Hervey, John, *The American Trotter*. New York: Coward McCann, 1947.

Hildreth, Samuel C., *Spell of the Turf*. Philadelphia: Lippincott, 1926.

Hunt, Frazier and Robert, *Horses and Heroes*. New York: Scribner's, 1949.

Johnston, Charles H. L., *Famous Cavalry Leaders*. Boston: 1908.

Linsley, Daniel C., *Morgan Horses*. New York: Saxton, 1857.

Luce, Edward A., *Keogh, Comanche, and Custer*. Dedham, Mass.: 1939.

Marshall, John, *Life of George Washington*. Philadelphia: Wayne, 1804.

The New York Times: Sport sections 1918-74, selected years.

Roe, Frank G., *The Indian and the Horse*. Norman, Oklahoma: University of Oklahoma Press, 1955.

Self, Margaret C., *The Horseman's Encyclopedia*. New York: Barnes, 1946.

Sheridan, Philip H., *Personal Memoirs*. New York: Webster, 1888.

Speed, John G., *The Horse in America*. New York: McClure, 1905.

Stong, Philip D., *Horses and Americans*. New York: Stokes, 1939.

Thayer, Bert Clark, *Whirlaway*. New York: Duell, 1946.

Thomason, John W., Jr., *Jeb Stuart*. New York: Scribner's, 1930.

U. S. Cavalry Association, *The Cavalry Journal*. Washington: 1936.

Willett, Peter, *The Thoroughbred*. New York: Putnam, 1970.

Wyman, Walter D., *The Wild Horse of the West*. Caldwell, Idaho: Caxton, 1945.